D1714406

THE GARDENER'S CALENDAR
for South-Carolina,
Georgia, & North-Carolina

THE GARDENER'S CALENDAR

for
South-Carolina,
Georgia, and North-Carolina

BY
ROBERT SQUIBB

Foreword by J. Kirkland Moore

Brown Thrasher Books
THE UNIVERSITY OF GEORGIA PRESS
Athens

First published in 1787 in Charleston, South Carolina

Foreword by J. Kirkland Moore copyright © 1980 by the
University of Georgia Press, Athens, Georgia 30602

Set in 12 on 14 point Mergenthaler Janson
Printed in the United States of America

Library of Congress Catalog Card Number 79-5191
International Standard Book Number 0-8203-0497-2

CONTENTS

FOREWORD

O F ROBERT SQUIBB's years in England we
know very little, but we may safely assume
from his subsequent career that Mr. Squibb was well
versed in the science of botany as well as in the less
genteel science of "dunging and hoeing." He arrived
in Charleston, South Carolina, in 1780 and immediately applied for American citizenship, which he obtained in 1783. Five years after his arrival, in 1785,
Squibb leased a large plot of ground on Meeting
Street near Rumney Bridge and there opened a nursery; he was soon to become one of Charleston's most
successful businessmen. Advertisements for his nursery appeared regularly in the "South Carolina Ga-
zette," and Squibb's name was often mentioned in
contemporary British journals since he was responsible for introducing rare American plants to British
gardens. At the time Squibb opened his nursery, the
South Carolina planters were organizing a society to
promote the interests of agriculture, and Robert

vii

Squibb was naturally one of the charter members. In 1787 Squibb published *The Gardener's Calendar for South-Carolina, Georgia, and North-Carolina*, dedicating his book to this esteemed group of planters who in Squibb's words were responsible for "promoting and improving agricultural and other rural concerns."

Squibb's *Gardener's Calendar* followed a format commonly found in eighteenth-century British and French gardening texts. Written to be read chronologically by month, it was to serve as a planting guide for gardeners in the South. *The Gardener's Calendar* tells the reader in detail not only what to plant each month of the year, but how to cultivate properly for the best possible results. Most British calendars were not so detailed as Squibb's. As an example, for the month of January Squibb suggested that of all the beans the southern gardener could plant the Windsor was the best sort, and he wrote that it should be planted in the first week of the month, either with a blunt-end dibble or in drills two or three inches deep. From this example it should be obvious to the modern-day reader how important Squibb's *Gardener's Calendar* was to the eighteenth-century southern gardener. For the first time our gardening ancestor had in black and white the proper method for the cultivation of vegetables and fruits in his own climate and region explained by a professional nurseryman. No longer must he guess about the effects of the difference in climate between Georgia and the Carolinas and England.

The popularity of Squibb's calendar ranged

widely. Copies could have been found in libraries both public and private from New England to Florida. In 1789 Squibb decided to publish a second edition, but it was not released to the public until 1809, three years after Squibb's death at Silk Hope Plantation near Savannah. The most widely known edition was printed in 1827. Since this edition was not printed by subscription only, as were the previous editions, it was read by a much larger and widely scattered audience.

If we look back in time, long before Robert Squibb arrived in Charleston, we know that in almost every instance the evolution of gardens and gardening followed a natural and possibly predictable progression. In the seventeenth century in North Carolina and South Carolina this progression without exception started with simple gardens intended to provide food, and these gardens also furnished seeds and nursery stock for sale to new settlers who arrived to begin their own agricultural operations. The most common problem facing the early planters was a lack of information about the cultivation of garden plants in the new world. English gardening books were not written with the Carolina climate and soil in mind.

For a full generation the early colonists blindly developed a new agricultural system by trial and error, and by experimentation these brave, persevering men and women built the foundation for what was to become in the next century a culturally and economically sound plantation society. In time colonial Carolina's two main crops, rice and indigo, succeeded to the financial benefit of the planters. While the planters' wealth was increasing, the political situation in the Carolinas also changed when a new colony named after George II of England was established on the vulnerable southern border of South Carolina, which now benefited from its protection. The creation of Georgia changed the complexion of the Carolina low country, and with new security on their borders planters here became the most influential and independent people of the region. With their increasing wealth, they bought books and luxuries, and their slaves gave them leisure to read and carry out philosophical and agricultural experiments.

"Botanick gardens" were all the rage in mid-eighteenth-century Charleston. Large plots of ground securely walled with brick or palings became exotic hideaways for the pressured merchant or planter. The earliest documented garden of this type was owned and cared for by a Mrs. Lamboll, on the extreme southwest end of King Street in Charleston. The garden was richly furnished with flowers and botanical curiosities as well as all the common vegetables needed for family use. Mrs. Lamboll was followed by Mrs. Logan, who cultivated an extensive garden in the same area of Charleston. Mrs. Logan was the daughter of Robert Daniel, one of the last proprietary governors of colonial South Carolina, and was married to George Logan, a Scotsman who settled in South Carolina in 1690. Mrs. Logan, at the age of seventy, transcribed all the knowledge she had acquired by long years of experience and observation. After her death this compendium of garden knowledge was published, entitled *The Gardener's Kalendar*.

John Watson was Charleston's most respected gardener in the middle eighteenth century. He came to Charleston to assist Henry Laurens in developing his botanical garden, and stayed there to open the first nursery in the region. He offered for sale a large variety of seeds and plants both domestic and imported, as well as all the necessary garden tools. The ravages of the Revolutionary War destroyed Watson's attempts at becoming the South's first successful plantsman. Watson's garden was revived and continued after the peace of 1783, but lost importance because of the increasing competition.

Thanks to Mr. Watson and the nameless others, the gardeners of the eighteenth-century Carolinas and Georgia were never dependent on northern seedsmen for necessary garden supplies, as were the Middle Atlantic colonies. The publicity received in the local gazettes by the local nurserymen and the almost obsessed amateur gardener spread the fascination of gardens and gardening all over Georgia and the Carolinas. Clubs and societies were formed where at meetings plants and new and exciting information were traded, in some cases putting local nurserymen out of business. It was into this world of intense agricultural interest that Robert Squibb arrived when he stepped off the boat at Charleston in 1780. Here was a world that could well use his skills and talents, and he prospered in it.

FOREWORD

I first became acquainted with Mr. Squibb's *Gardener's Calendar* while working on a garden restoration project for Colonial Williamsburg in 1976. Though the garden I was researching predated 1760, the 1787 edition of *The Gardener's Calendar* did help to establish the existence of certain British vegetable types in America in the eighteenth century, and more importantly in the South. Added to that, Mr. Squibb's detailed directions for the cultivation of eighteenth-century vegetables allowed me to instruct the Colonial Williamsburg gardeners on how to cultivate the restored vegetable gardens creating an authentic effect.

My knowing of Squibb's *Calendar* was the result of sheer luck, and locating a copy of the 1787 edition was even more unlikely as there are fewer than five copies known to exist. It is hoped that this accurate new edition will make it possible for museums, restorations, and historical societies in the South to reexamine their restored or reconstructed gardens and make the necessary changes, following Squibb's guidance; or this book may help defend long-established but poorly documented historical fact. Beyond this special use, I would also hope that the contemporary gardener of the South will find not only pleasure but instruction as well in reading Mr. Squibb's *Calendar*. It is a delightful book for all who love gardens and gardening.

J. KIRKLAND MOORE

Isle of Hope
  Savannah, Georgia

xii

THE
GARDENER's CALENDAR,
FOR
SOUTH-CAROLINA, GEORGIA,
AND
NORTH-CAROLINA.

CONTAINING

An Account of Work neceſſary to be done in the KITCHEN and FRUIT GARDENS every month in the year, with Inſtructions for performing the ſame.

Alſo particular Directions relative to SOIL and SITU-ATION, adapted to the different Kinds of Plants and Trees moſt proper for Cultivation in theſe States.

By ROBERT SQUIBB,
NURSERY AND SEEDSMAN OF CHARLESTON, SOUTH-CAROLINA.

CHARLESTON:

Printed by SAMUEL WRIGHT and Co. for R. SQUIBB, and Recorded in the SECRETARY OF STATE's Office, agreeable to the Act of Aſſembly.

[Price Six Shillings.]
M DCC LXXXVII.

[facsimile of the 1787 title page]

To the Honorable

THOMAS HEYWARD, ESQ.
President;

THOMAS PINCKNEY, ESQ.
Vice-President;
and to

THE OTHER MEMBERS
of the South-Carolina Society,
for Promoting and Improving Agriculture,
and Other Rural Concerns.

GENTLEMEN,

THE PATRONAGE you have given to the follow-ing Sheets, by permitting me to dedicate them to such Respectable Characters, whose concurient Ex-ertions, like the fertilizing Nile, thus happily coin-cide to promote more diffusively the real Interests of our Country, will ever be considered by me, with the deepest sense of gratitude and esteem.

The Art of Agriculture having been the principal part of my Study through life, as it is my Duty as a Member of your Society, so shall I ever think it the highest Point of my Ambition to be allowed to throw in my little Mite of Information, whereby I may, in any Degree, be instrumental in forwarding the End of your most laudable Institution.

That your Endeavours may prosper, and Agricul-ture succeed; that Industry may prevail, and every

useful Art flourish throughout these United States,
is the earnest Wish of, Gentlemen,
                    Your most devoted,
                    and obedient
                        humble Servant,
                            ROBERT SQUIBB

INTRODUCTION

GARDENING at the perfection to which it has been advanced, in many parts of the world, is entitled to a place of considerable rank among the liberal Arts.

As there is no doubt that with care and attention, almost every species of vegetables may be propagated in this climate to as great perfection as in any part of the universe; it is to be hoped that every improvement which can possibly be suggested, in the infant state of Horticulture in this country, will meet with every possible degree of encouragement; more especially when we call to mind the many necessaries and conveniencies of life which are derived to us from the produce of the garden; and how superabundantly the assiduous labourer is here rewarded by the exuberance of vegetation.

Under such persuasion, and from the repeated solicitations of many reputable characters in this and the adjoining States, R. SQUIBB has been induced to submit to the perusal of the Public the following Epitom of GARDENING, which is founded on experience and observation.

This being his first Essay, he flatters himself that the candid Public will overlook any trifling mistake or inaccuracy that may possibly occur to their notice; and the more so, as his attention (since the commencement of the undertaking) has been greatly diverted, through the urgent application of his friends, to the pursuit of his manual profession; and his feeble efforts in the intervals only have been exerted to point out, in a plain, concise and familiar manner, the most beneficial rules (to the utmost of his practice, knowledge and abilities) peculiarly adapted to the climate, and most agreeable to the general system of Horticulture, throughout every month in the year—in doing of which he candidly acknowledges to have followed, as much as possible, the method and style of a justly admired European Gardener.

However mysterious some propositions in this work may appear to his readers respecting foreign seeds, and some other deviations from the usual practice, which the variation of climate makes necessary; let them be assured, that what is here laid down, has been the result of much experience, which no theorical ideas can confute—he having studied with attention, the soils and seasons, best calculated for sowing and planting the most useful vegetables, &c. adapted for, or peculiar to this country.

JANUARY

Work to be done in the Kitchen Garden

 BEANS

IN THE BEGINNING of this month, if the weather is open, let some ground be got ready for a principal crop of broad beans. The best sorts are—

The windsor bean, sandwich bean, toker bean, &c.

The windsor bean is an excellent sort, and may be planted the first week in this month; also the toker, which is very fine, and a good bearer. Let the rows be four feet distant from each other; and set the beans either with a blunt ended dibble, two or three inches deep, or drill them that depth; and about five or six inches asunder in the rows.

3

If you have not planted any mazagon and long podded beans before this month; let some of the two sorts be planted as early as possible—you may plant the mazagon, long podded, and windsor beans all at the same time; and they will succeed each other in bearing.

The mazagon bean should be planted in rows two feet asunder, and four inches distant in the rows; and the long pods two feet and a half or three feet from row to row, and six or seven inches in the row.

 PEAS

Let some early hotspur peas be sown the beginning of this month for a full crop, in a warm piece of ground, to succeed the same sorts sown in the two last months—the sorts are—

Charleton, hotspur, golden hotspur, Essex hotspur, &c. but the two first are the earliest, and the other is proper to succeed them; sow each sort in rows four feet asunder; if the ground is rich, and you intend to set sticks for their support—but, if you do not intend to give them sticks, three feet will be sufficient.

At the same time also you may sow the first crop of marrowfat peas, and they will succeed the hotspur, for they will come into bearing as the others go off. This pea is much admired in most families; but the dwarf marrowfat is the properest for sowing at this season; observing, if you intend to set sticks for those peas to run upon, to sow them in rows five feet distant from each other—but, if no sticks are intended, three feet and a half will afford space enough.

If you have pease and beans, already advanced two or three inches high or more, take the advantage of a fine day, when the surface of the ground is dry, and draw some earth up to their stems.

This should not be omitted; for it will strengthen the plants, and protect them greatly against the frost and wind.

 CABBAGES

About the beginning, middle, or any time in this month, you may sow early York, sugar-loaf and drum-head cabbage-seed, to come in for summer use —for this purpose, chuse a warm border, under a wall or fence—Dig the ground a spade deep, throw it up into a bed or beds, sow the seed pretty thick, and rake the surface even—should severe weather set in, you may throw a little light litter or straw over the beds, before or after the plants are up.

If your cabbage-plants, sown in October or November, were not transplanted last month, let them be put out soon in this. Let the ground be well manured with good rotten dung, and dig it in a full spade deep, if the land will bear it. Rake the ground smooth, and plant your drumhead or large cabbage plants two feet and a half distant from row to row, and the same distance in the rows . . . [See December.]

 CAULIFLOWERS

Let every care be taken to protect your cauliflowers from frost—This may be done by binding moss or hay bands round the stems, and about one third of the leaves, and tying the leaves together near the tops.

About the middle of this month, you may transplant the cauliflowers sown in October, if they are of full size to transplant. Let these plants be put out into a warm situation, and in a spot of rich soil well manured with good rotten dung; and plant them about two feet and a half distant from row to row, and two feet in the rows.

 BROCCOLI

Let your broccoli have frequent hoeings; and let the decayed leaves be taken away as they fall off, which are no ways pleasing to the eye.

 TURNIPS

About the latter end of this month, sow a few dutch turnips, for an early crop—if they succeed they will come in about the beginning of April, and will be exceeding good.

6

JANUARY

 BEETS

Sow beets about the latter end of this month, of different sorts, the red beet for a large root, and the green and white sorts, for their leaves in soup, stewing, &c.

Beet seed being pretty large it is an eligible method, either to sow it in drills, in order that it may be more regularly buried in the earth, at an equal depth; or to dot it in with a blunt ended dibble in rows—Let the drills be drawn with a hoe, about an inch and a half deep, and ten or twelve inches asunder—Divide the ground into beds five feet wide, put three or four seeds into each hole, and cover them in as you go on; and after the plants are come up some time, leave only one of the strongest in each hole.

It will be most proper to sow the red and the other sorts separate; for it is the root of the red sort only that is used; and the leaves of the white and green kinds.

 CARROTS

When the weather is mild and dry, at any time in this month, let a warm spot of ground be prepared for a few early carrots—Dig the ground a full spade deep, and break the earth well as you go on.

This is only intended for a few to come in a little before the general crop; therefore only a small piece of ground should be prepared for this purpose—

7

Choose a dry mild day to sow the seed; and you may sow a thin sprinkling of radishes with the carrots; and let them be raked in soon; always observing to divide the ground into beds from four to five feet in width.

 ONIONS

Let your onions have frequent hoeings; and let the surface of the ground be constantly kept loose, which will greatly promote their growth.

 SPINAGE

On a small spot of ground you may sow a little spinage, to come early in the spring, at which time it will be very acceptable in most families; the smooth-leaved or round seeded is the best to sow at this season.

The seed may be sown about the middle or toward the latter end of this month, either in the broad cast, and raked in; or in broad, flat, shallow drills, drawn with a hoe flatways, about an inch deep, and a foot asunder; or you may sow it in drills between rows of early beans and peas.

 PARSLEY

Sow some parsley seed in open weather, about the middle or towards the end of this month.

8

JANUARY

There are two kinds of parsley, the common plain, and curl-leaved, but the latter is greatly to be pre-fered; the leaves being large, thick, and bushy, and excellent for culinary uses, and much admired for garnish to dishes. Let shallow drills be drawn in a dry part of the garden, and sow the seeds therein pretty thick, and cover them about half an inch deep with earth.

These seeds may be sown in a single drill round the edges of the kitchen garden quarters, or along the edges of the borders next the paths—This seed lies in the ground sometimes a month or six weeks before it makes its appearance.

 LETTUCES

Transplant some more lettuces from the beds or bor-ders where they stand too close together—In doing this, observe to draw the plants out regularly, and let the strongest remain in the bed or border ten or twelve inches distance; then loosen the surface of the earth with a hoe, and clear away the weeds and litter.

The plants which are taken out, should be planted in a warm border of rich earth, at ten or twelve inches distance each way; and if the weather is dry let them have a little water.

Cabbage, silesia, and Dutch brown lettuce may be sown at any time in this month in a sheltered situa-tion, in a spot of light rich earth, open to the sun.

Pick off all dead and decayed leaves as they appear

on the plants, and keep them perfectly clear of weeds; and if you stir the surface of the earth between the plants sometimes it will be of service to them.

 CELLERY

When the weather is open take the advantage of a dry day to earth up such cellery as require it.

Let the earth be well broken and laid up to the plants lightly, that they may not be crushed down or bruised, raising the earth near to the top of the plants; should severe frost set in, it will injure part of the tops of the plants that are above ground; and if much of the plants should be out of ground in such weather, and be thereby destroyed, it will also occasion a decay of those parts that are within the ground—Therefore it may be necessary to cover the rows with long litter, straw, &c.

 ENDIVE

In dry open weather let some of the full grown endive be prepared for blanching—take the opportunity of a fine day, when the plants are quite dry, and tie the leaves of each plant together; and with a small hoe draw up some earth round them seperately, to assist their whitening, and to protect them more effectually from the frost—They will be blanched for use in a fortnight proper for sallads, soup, stewing, &c. [For further information see December.]

JANUARY

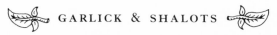 GARLICK & SHALOTS

If your garlick or shalots are not already planted, the business should be no longer omitted.—[See October.]

 RADISHES

In the beginning, or any time this month when the weather is open and mild, sow some short top radishes for an early crop, on a warm border that lies well to the sun, under a wall or fence—and about the latter end you may sow the same sort, and some salmon radishes, to succeed them.

You should not mix both sorts together, but let each sort be sown by itself, for the short top will come in ten or twelve days sooner than the salmon radishes; and the short top are much more hardy than the salmon—

The surest method is to sow some short top at least twice or oftner in this month—therefore if you sow some about the beginning, and again at the middle, and towards the latter end of the month, in a warm situation you will seldom fail of success.

There may be mixed and sown with the radishes a sprinkling of carrot seed; for if the radishes should fail, the carrots may succeed; and if both succeed, there will be a double advantage—for when the radishes are drawn off for use, there remains a crop of carrots, which will come in at an early period; or, instead of carrots, you may sow a little lettuce seed or round spinage, and when the radishes are gone off these will come in.

You should sow your radish seeds pretty thick at this season; for when the radish seeds begin to appear, if the weather should prove sharp, it will cut some off, and the birds too will be apt to attack them and destroy many; sow the seeds regularly over the surface, and throw the ground up into beds, about four or four feet and a half wide, and rake the surface even, standing in the alleys—Should there be any appearance of frost after the seed is sown, it will be proper to spread some dry straw or litter over the surface an inch or two thick; which will keep the surface warm, prevent the injury of the frost, and greatly forward the germination of the seed—

Likewise when the plants begin to appear, the same precaution will be necessary to protect them from the frost, by spreading a little straw or litter over the surface, there to remain till they are fairly up—and if the weather proves frosty afterwards, cover them with a little straw, or some light ever green bushes, which may be continued occasionally; by which means the plants will be greatly forwarded in their growth: for should cold north west winds prevail in the day time, the bushes will break the wind, which is almost as hurtful to them as the frost: but this covering must not by any means be kept on in mild, but only in severe weather, until the plants are fairly in rough leaves.

JANUARY

 ARTICHOKES

Where your Artichokes were not dressed and landed up in the last month, let this work be done now as soon as possible.—[For the method see October.]

 ASPARAGUS

If your Asparagus beds were not dressed in the last month, let this business be attended to soon in this.—[See October.]

 HORSE RADISH

This plant is propagated by cuttings, either taken off the top an inch or two long, or from the old roots cut in pieces of that length—but the top or crown of the plant is most preferable. The method is this—

First procure a quantity of proper sets;—which may be either the small off-sets that arise from the sides of the main roots, of which take cuttings off their tops, an inch or two long; or you may use the tops of the crowns of the old roots, when taken up for use: or in default of a sufficiency of crowns or tops of either, you may divide a quantity of old knotty roots into cuttings of two inches long; which, if furnished each with two or three buds or eyes, will make tollerable sets. When you intend to make a fresh plantation, you should, during the winter, when you take up the plants for use, reserve all the best crowns

13

of the main roots for planting. But this latter practice can only be pursued in private gardens: for where the large roots are for sale, their tops must not be taken off, which would render them unsaleable in market: therefore the Market Gardeners reserve the strongest off-sets arising from the main root.

Being thus furnished with a proper quantity of sets, proceed to prepare the ground for their reception. And they may either be planted with a dibble, after the ground is dug; or trenched in, as you proceed in digging the ground.

Choose an open situation, and as light and deep a soil as the Garden affords; which must be trenched regularly one good spade deep at least; but if the ground will admit of it, the deeper it is loosened the better.

Then proceed by dibble planting, in the following manner, being provided with a long dibble, begin at one end of the piece of ground—range the line crossways; and with the dibble make holes about fifteen inches deep; and be careful to make them all of an equal depth; which you may readily do by making a mark upon the dibble, and so thrusting it down to that mark: makeing the holes six inches asunder, dropping as you go on, one set or cutting into each hole, with the crown, &c. upwards; taking care to fill or close the hole properly with earth—the rows to be one foot six inches asunder.

The other method of planting, by trenching in the sets, is to open a trench at one end, in the common method of trenching, two spades wide and one spade deep or more; and then having the sets or cuttings provided, plant one row along the bottom of the trench with the crowns upright, about six inches asunder; then dig the next trench the same depth and width, turning the earth into the first trench, over the row of sets; thus proceed, trench after trench, to the end.

By practicing either of the above methods of planting horse-radish, the sets will put forth perfectly straight-rooted shoots quite to the top, whereby they will be long and smooth, and swell evenly their whole length, and will sometimes attain a tolerable perfection the first summer's growth.

When the whole is planted, the ground may be sown with spinage or radishes, which will come off time enough to give the horse radish full time to grow —for these will not come up till the first or middle of April, when the spinage and radishes will be all gathered.

They must be kept weeded for a month or six weeks, after which the leaves will cover the ground, and prevent the growth of weeds.

In the autumn after planting, or about michael-mas, you may begin to take up some of the roots, if wanted for use: but it will be adviseable to let the principal part remain, to have another summer's growth, when they will be very fine and large.

When you take up these roots, it should be done regularly—not digging up a stick here and there, as is often practised in private gardens; but beginning at the first row, and so proceeding from row to row, according as you want them: observing to throw out a trench close along the first row of roots, and as deep as the roots go, but not to loosen the bottom or old set from whence these proceed, which is called the stool.

Having thus cleared away the earth quite close to the stool or bottom of the roots, then with a knife cut each root off level, close to the stool from whence it proceeds—for all the stools or bottoms of the roots must be left in the ground undisturbed; for these will yield a supply of fine roots, the succeeding year— and when the roots are dug up, the stools still remaining will continue as often as the produce is gathered, to furnish a fresh supply of roots every succeeding year.

But care must be taken, when digging up the roots, always to clear the old stool from all straggling or small roots whatever; and in the summer season to draw up all the small plants rising between the rows.

The Fruit Garden

PEACH, NECTARINE, & APRICOT TREES

Pruning may be performed on these Trees any time in this month.

JANUARY

In doing this business, you are to observe, that although the trees were pruned last summer, there will still remain many branches which ought to be taken out—The most irregular and most abundant of them are to be cut away, and a due supply of the best-placed and most moderate, strong shoots are to be preserved, in every part, at proper distances—For these trees produce their fruit principally from their former summer's shoots.

The old naked branches, having no young shoots on them, should be entirely taken out; which you will frequently meet with in old standard trees; particularly in their lower and middle limbs. The cause is chiefly owing to neglect of pruning, in due season; for the upper branches crowding over the lower and middle ones, destroy their fertility.

Therefore in pruning these trees, let some of the old naked wood be cut away in every winter's pruning, to make room for the last summer's shoots; and where the branches of the trees are too crowded, let them be thined; observing to take off such as grow most irregularly: and when any branches run across, or interfere much with any of the others, in an improper direction, let them be cut out. But a due supply should be left every where, at moderate distances, to bear fruit the next summer; and all such as are not wanted must be cut away quite close, leaving only the short spurs.

The weaker shoots, which are now left, must, at the same time, be shortened, more or less, according

17

to the vigour of the tree, and strength of the different shoots; which is done in order to procure an effectual supply of new shoots next year, to bear fruit the year following.

But in shortening the shoots, mind to proportion every one, according to it's growth, and original length. For instance—A shoot of about a foot long, may be shortened to six or seven inches, according to it's strength; and one from fifteen to eighteen inches, may be shortened to about twelve; and one from two to three feet, need not be shortened at all, if the strength is in proportion to it's length. And you will even find sometimes shoots of a foot long that require no shortening, observing always to leave the strongest and largest shoots.

The general rule for shortening the shoots of young trees, after the first year's planting, is, if they are very strong and vigorous, you may shorten them one fourth; if pretty strong, one third; and if weak, cut off two thirds. Observe to prune out side branches, that are above an inch long; and leave none but the main shoots on the trees—As to the number of the branches, I refer you to heading down young trees. —[See March.]

But such peach, nectarine, and apricot trees, as produce strong and vigorous shoots must be treated accordingly, and must also be shortened less in proportion; and the stronger the branches are, the more room they should have.—When the tree is pruned, the branches should be at least from sixteen to eighteen inches distant from each other, at the extremity of each shoot; but indeed some of the most vigorous shoots should not be shortened at all—This is the only method of pruning, to bring a vigorous shooting tree in good order, so as to produce moderate shoots, such as will bear fruit.

For the more wood you cut out, and in proportion as the shoots are shortened, the more vigorous the trees will become.

By what I have above hinted, the pruner will not be at a loss to know in what manner peach, nectarine, and apricot trees, according to their different growth are to be treated. In the article of pruning, the rule here mentioned is always to be applied to winter prunings.

Another thing is also proper to be observed; that is, where any young shoots, which are left to bear, have produced only small shoots from their sides, they must be cut off close to the principal, for those will neither produce good fruit, nor good wood.

It is proper to direct also, in shortening the shoots, to cut them off as much as possible at a leaf or wood bud, distinguishable from the blossom buds, by being long and flat; the others being round and swelling: or otherwise to prune to a twain blossom bud, that is where two buds arise at the same eye, having a wood bud between them. Either of these rules are necessary to be observed in shortening; in order that each may produce a leading shoot next summer, forming a leader to the main shoot. For where there is a fair leading shoot provided near the extremity of a bearing branch, such shoot seldom fails to yield a fair and well flavoured fruit.

It will be also necessary to remark one thing more in pruning of these trees; particularly the apricot—In this tree we often perceive in the two year old branches, some short shoots or spurs, on which are frequently to be seen several blossom buds: now some people cut these spurs entirely off, but I am much against such practice; for some of these short natural spurs will produce handsome fruit, both in apricots, peaches, and nectarines, but especially the former.

TRANSPLANT FRUIT TREES

At any time in this month you may with great safety transplant any kinds of fruit trees.—[For the work see December.]

Support tall new planted fruit trees with stakes as soon as they are planted, that they may not be rocked about by the wind, which would greatly retard them from taking root.

VINES

Vines may be pruned at any time in this month, if not done in the two former ones.—[For the method see December.]

You may still continue to prune apple, pear,

plumb, and cherry trees, if not done in the former month—[For the work see December.]

 PRUNING RASBERRY PLANTS

Prune rasberries—In doing this let it be observed, that all the old wood that produced fruit last summer must now be cut out; for these never bear but once. —Therefore a supply of young wood must be left to bear next year; observe therefore to leave several of the strongest of the last summer's shoots standing upon every root, to bear the fruit to be expected next year.—These being the only proper bearing shoots, they must be allowed room; therefore as above hinted, let all the old wood be cut close to the ground; and selecting from three to five of the best young shoots on each root or stool, let all the rest above that number be cut away close to the surface of the earth; and at the same time let all straggling roots be destroyed.

Each of the shoots that are left to bear must be shortened—the rule is this.—Take off one third or one fourth or thereabouts of the original length of each shoot, according to the different growths.

In dressing, observe to take up and clear away all straggling roots between the rows, and also all such as do not belong to the standing plants; this digging will strengthen the roots, and the ground will lie clean and neat all the winter.

PLANT RASBERRIES

This is a good season to plant rasberries.—When a new plantation is wanted, observe that the young shoots or suckers which arise every summer from the old roots are the most proper plants for the propagation of them: and fresh plantations of these shrubs should be made in an open situation, where the ground is good; and if you dig in some dung it will be of advantage to the plants.

In choosing the plants for this plantation, observe to take such as are well furnished with roots, for that is a principal article in rasberry plants; and if there be but one or two or more buds formed on the root for next summer shoots, such plants are particularly to be chosen.

Having procured the plants, shorten the shoots a little, and leave only one of the strongest shoots on each root—Let the ends of the roots be also trimmed; then put the plants in rows four or five feet distant, and let them be planted half a yard distant from each other in the rows.

FEBRUARY

Work to be done in the Kitchen Garden

 BEANS

PLANT BEANS of any kind; for all sorts will succeed from this planting.

This is still a proper season for the windsor, toker, and also the long pod bean, which is a very great bearer.—Any of the small kind of beans may be planted in this month.

Some of the most approved sorts of beans should be put into the ground every fortnight or three weeks; which will afford a regular supply of young beans during the season for them.

Plant the windsor and toker in rows about three feet and a half, and the long pods about three feet asunder.

23

 PEAS

Sow marrowfat, sugar, rounceval, and other sorts of pease once a fortnight or three weeks; by which means you will have a constant succession of young peas for the table.

Any other of the large or smaller sorts of peas, as mentioned in the former months, may be now sown, allowing the distance of three weeks or thereabouts between each sowing.

Draw drills or trenches for the different kinds of peas, as mentioned in the former months; and sow them regularly, and cover them over with earth about three inches deep.

All sorts of pease should be sown in open situations, but by no means under trees.

Draw the earth to such pease and beans as are now up some height; it will strengthen the plants greatly, and will encourage their growth.

 SOW CABBAGE SEED

About the beginning of this month, is a very good season for sowing cabbage seeds to come in for summer use;—for those which were sown last month are very apt to be cut off by the frost, if they are not properly protected with straw, matts, or evergreen bushes.

The sorts proper to sow now, are the early York, sugar-loaf, and all the large kinds.

FEBRUARY

Let a part of the south border of your garden, if vacant, be prepared to receive the seeds, and divide it into beds crossways the border, three or four feet wide, and sow the seeds thereon but not too thick; for it is intended that those plants should remain there till they are fit to put out for good.—In dry weather let them be frequently watered, and observe to do it always in the morning as soon after sun-rise as possible.

 CABBAGES

Transplant cabbage plants of all kinds, if not done in the former month, in the places where they are to remain to cabbage.—It may be done at any time in this month; but if the plants be strong and in good order, the sooner it is done the better: Let them be planted in good ground; allowing about two or two and a half feet distance for the York and sugar-loaf, and two and a half or three feet for the larger sorts.

This distance is to be understood of such plants as are to remain to grow to their full size; but such of the forward kinds as are to be cut while young, may be planted closer; and sixteen or eighteen inches apart will be sufficient.

Plant out also red cabbages, if not done in the last month; allow two feet distance in the row, and two feet or two feet and a half between row and row.

 CAULIFLOWERS

If your cauliflowers sown in October, were not planted out in the last month, let it be done soon in this; and plant them in a good rich soil in a warm situation, in rows at about two feet and a half distance from row to row, and two feet from each other in the row.

 LETTUCES

Transplant lettuce plants from the beds or borders where they have stood all the winter, that is, if they stand too close.

The plants which are drawn out should be planted in an open spot of rich ground, at ten or twelve inches distance each way.—If the weather be dry let them be watered.—[See January.]

Lettuce seeds of different sorts should be sown the beginning of this month, for a general crop; and to have a regular supply, let some more be sown about the middle, and again towards the latter end of the month.

The proper sorts of lettuce, to sow at this time, are the white coss, the green coss, cabbage, Silesia, brown Dutch; or in short any sorts may be now sown.

Dig, for these seeds, a rich spot of ground, in an open situation; and let the earth be well broken; sow the seeds on the surface, with an even hand; and rake them in lightly, taking care not to draw the earth in heaps.

FEBRUARY

 SPINAGE

Sow spinage to succeed that sown in the last month; the sowings should be repeated every fortnight, or three weeks, or thereabout, to have a regular supply; for the produce of each will not continue fit for use much longer, before it will run.—Let the seed be of the round leaved or smooth seeded kind; which is the most proper sort to sow at this season; its leaves being considerably thicker, and every way larger than the prickly spinage.

The seed may at this season be sown either in a spot alone, or with other crops; particularly, between rows of windsor beans, or between cabbages, or with radishes, &c. observing that, either alone or with other crops, spinage seed should be sown pretty thick, and generally in the broad cast.—Let it be evenly raked.—Or you may otherwise sow it in broad flat drills, about a foot wide, near an inch deep, and a foot asunder.

Let it be observed that spinage should not at this season, be sown, in a situation which is much shaded with trees or bushes; for in such case it is probable the plants would be drawn up to seed, before they arrive to half their growth.

Hoe, or hand-weed early crops of spring spinage, thinning the plants at the same time, to five or six inches distance.

The crops of winter spinage, which were sown last autumn, will be now advancing to good perfection for use; and should be now kept clean from weeds, and the earth between the plants stirred with a hoe; and, in gathering the plants for use, if they stand close you should pull them out clean by the roots; but if they already stand at wide distances, only crop the larger outward leaves as wanted, 'till they begin to run; then cut them up clean at the bottom.

 ONIONS AND LEEKS

I would recommend that onions may be sown this month for a general crop. But I am well aware that many may be of a different opinion, and may perhaps condemn me for attempting a matter so contrary to the usual practice. Therefore I hope that I shall not be rashly accused, before my method is fairly tried.

The beginning of this month, prepare a piece of good rich ground; and let it be well manured, and dug a full spade deep; and throw the square into beds, about four feet over; and let the alleys be about one foot wide, and four inches deep.—Draw four drills or trenches on each bed, at equal distances, about half an inch deep; scatter the seed thinly in each trench, and cover it with the back side of the rake, and then rake it over evenly, standing in the alleys.

Let your transplanted onions have frequent hoeings, and never suffer the surface of the earth to be bound, but kept constantly loose.—Leeks may be sown and managed in the like manner.

FEBRUARY

 RADISHES

Sow some radish seeds, to have a fresh supply to succeed those sown in last month.—There should be
some of the salmon, short top, and turnip radishes
sown at two or three different times in this month;
that is—at the beginning, middle, and latter end; by
which means there will be a due succession of young
radishes for the table.—Let this seed be now sown in
an open spot, where the ground is good, and rather of
a light, pliable nature.

In sowing these seeds observe the method as mentioned in the last month.

Thin the crops of early radishes, as soon as they
arrive to the size of a goose quill; which will greatly
promote the growth of the small plants; observe to
keep them free from weeds, and clear from any litter.

In dry weather, let the early crops of radishes be
frequently watered; otherwise they will not swell
freely, but will be sticky and hot.

 CARROTS AND PARSNIPS

Sow carrots and parsnips the beginning of this
month, for a principal crop; the carrots sown now
will be fit for use in May, June, July, and August.—
In the latter months you will find them very acceptable.

A spot of light deep ground, in an open situation,
should be chosen for carrots and parsnips; for the
roots will thrive best in such soil and situation.

29

The ground should be trenched one good spade deep at least; or rather double dig it, if the land will bear it. Observe in digging to take but thin spits; and be careful to break all the clods, that the roots may have full liberty to run down straight; for if the earth is not well divided or seperated, the roots will be apt to grow unkindly and forked.

Before you sow your seed, throw up the ground into beds, about four or five feet wide; and on each bed, draw four drills or trenches, and set the seed thin in each drill: or you may sow it in the broad cast method; you may also sprinkle a little radish seed amongst the carrots or parsnips, and rake the beds evenly, standing in the alleys.

DRESS OLD ASPARAGUS BEDS

About the beginning of this month let your asparagus beds have their spring dressing.—In the first place let all the weeds, &c. be cleared away from the surface of the beds; and having provided yourself with a three tined fork as described in October, let them be forked up and the surface laid smooth, and all the lumps of earth, if any, be beaten as fine as possible; —if the land is stubborn and will not rake just now, let it lie a few days and dry, and take the advantage of the first shower of rain, which will meliorate the soil so that the beds will rake free and easy: but before you have finished raking them, you may sow thereon some radish, spinage, or lettuce seed, which will not injure your asparagus in the least, provided you do not sow the seeds too thick. When this is done take all the stones, &c. out of the alleys, and if you can procure some dung let them be filled up within eight inches of the surface of the beds, and throw a little earth over it:—By the autumn this dung will be finally purified, and be of great service to the crop that you should plant on these beds, when it must be taken out and laid upon them.

SMALL SALLADING

Small sallading, such as cresses, mustard, radish, rape, &c. should, when a constant supply is wanted, be sown once in ten or twelve days, on a warm border, in drills about three or four inches asunder, let each sort be kept seperate, and cover them over lightly with fine earth.

When the plants begin to come up, if the earth should cake, so that they cannot rise freely, let it be broken lightly with the hand, or with a small rake.— If they should be attacked with frost, let them be watered before the sun comes on them, which will prevent their turning black, and spoiling.

CHERVIL AND CORIANDER

Sow chervil and coriander seeds.—Draw some shallow drills about ten inches or a foot asunder.—Sow each sort seperate; and cover them about an inch

31

deep with earth.—Those plants are all to remain where sown, till they come to perfection, and the chief culture they require is to keep them clear of weeds.

SOWING PARSLEY

Parsley, if not sown last month, may now be sown, either in beds; or in a single drill, at the edge of the quarters or borders of the garden; it will make a useful, and also a neat edging, if not suffered to grow rank, especially the curled parsley; or if large supplies are wanted for market, it may be sowed in continued rows, nine inches asunder; or upon the general surface, and raked in.

SOWING BASIL

Basil is, in some families, used as a kitchen herb.—it is propagated by seed; and the middle or latter end of this month, or early in March, is the season to sow it; and the plants will be ready for planting out in April.

POT, AND MEDICINAL HERBS

The seeds of dill, fennel, borage, burnet, bugloss, sorrel, marigold, orach, and clarey, together with the seeds of all other herbs of the like kinds, may be sowed any time this month, in a bed or border of common earth, and raked in; most of which you may let remain where sown, if the plants are properly thinned;—or you may transplant them into beds, a foot asunder, in April, or May.—plant slips of balm, burnet, tarragow, tansey, penny-royal, feverfew, and chamomile.

In taking off the slips of these plants, be careful to preserve some root to each if possible.—Plant them nine or ten inches distance from each other, in beds of rich earth.

Sow hysop, thyme, savory, and sweet marjoram, rather at the beginning; but they will succeed very well, if sown any time in this month. These seeds should be sown seperately, in spots of rich light earth, and raked in; or they may also be sown in shallow drills, along the edges of borders, or beds; covering them with fine earth, a quarter of an inch deep; and the plants will make neat and useful edgings.

These plants should remain where sown till October; at which time they should be thinned to five or six inches distance; and those that are drawn out may be planted in another spot, six inches asunder: those which are sown for edgings need not be thinned.

Plant slips of sage, hysop, thyme, and savory, any time in this month.

Those slips or cuttings should be of the last year's growth, from five to seven inches long, observing to slip or cut them off close to the place from whence they arise; but there are sometimes to be found slips or suckers arising from the bottom of the old plants, which are often furnished with roots: such slips or suckers should be particularly chosen.

Plant all sorts of these herbs in beds or borders, six or seven inches apart; they will take root, and become good plants in a short time.—Water them in dry weather, and they will be strong and well rooted; when they may be transplanted, at proper distances, in beds of rich earth.

 ROSEMARY, RUE, &c.

Plant slips of rosemary, rue, wormwood, and lavender; let these be planted in a shady border six inches asunder; they will take root freely if you observe to water them in dry weather: they may be transplanted into more open situations about October, when they will be strong and well rooted.

It must be observed also, in propagating the cuttings of these plants, that the shoots which were produced last year, are to be chosen for that purpose— They should be from five to seven inches in length, according as you can find them; observing to slip them off close to the part from whence they proceed.

Put each slip or cutting about two parts out of three into the ground.

But sometimes there are also slips or suckers to be met with, which arise immediately from the stems of the old plants, near the surface of the ground:— These should be prefered, because they are often well furnished with roots.

FEBRUARY

Now is a good time to make new plantations of Mint.

 MINT

This plant is to be propagated, either by parting the root, or by the slips of the young plants, taken up with roots or fibres at the bottom; or by the cuttings of the young stalks next month, or in April, &c. But at this season the increasing it by slips or parting the roots is most generally practiced—and the method is this:

Having procured the roots let them be planted in rows about six inches asunder, and five or six inches distant in the rows; and if the weather is dry let them have a tolerable watering, to settle the earth about their roots.

In the third or fourth week in this month you may have recourse to such old beds of mint, as are well stocked with plants; observing to slip or draw them up by the roots: In doing which, you must draw them up gently, and with the help of your knife at times, to raise or seperate them; by which care, every plant will rise with good roots.

The method of propogating by roots is this: Having procured a sufficient quantity of old roots, draw drills with a hoe six inches asunder, extend the roots or runners along the bottom of the drills; cover them about an inch deep with the earth, and then make the ground even.

 PLANTING ASPARAGUS

Any time in this month is a very proper season to remove the roots of asparagus, for the making of new plantations.

In the doing of which, the chief matter to be regarded is the choice of a proper soil; which should be the best and deepest the garden affords: it must not be too wet, nor too strong or stubborn; but such as is moderately light and pliable; so that it will readily fall to pieces in digging, raking, &c. and in a situation that is open, and enjoys the full sun.

The ground where you intend to make new asparagus beds should be regularly trenched or dug to a good depth; and a large quantity of rotten dung buried in each trench, at least ten or twelve inches below the surface of the ground.

The ground being dug and laid level, divide it into beds three feet in width, with alleys about twenty inches wide between bed and bed.

Two rows of these roots are to be planted on each bed, allowing about sixteen or eighteen inches between each plant; and let the rows be about eighteen inches from row to row.

Next let it be observed that the plants to be chosen must not be more than two years old; but most good gardeners prefer those that are only one year from the seed, which are such as I would recommend; as from experience I have found they have generally taken root more freely, and succeeded every way better than two year old plants.

The following is the method of planting them:

Strain your line length-ways the beds, about eight inches from the edge; and then, with a spade, cut out a small trench or drill, close to the line, about six inches deep; making that side next the line nearly upright; and when one trench is opened, plant that, before you open another, at the distance before directed.

In placing the roots observe they must not be horizontally extended or put flat in the bottom of the trench, as practiced by some people; but they must be laid nearly upright, against the back of the trench or drill, so that the crown of the plants may also stand upright, about two or three inches below the surface of the ground: Let them be all placed at an equal depth, spreading their roots a little in nearly a direct position against the back of the trench; and, at the same time, drawing a little earth up against them with the hand, as you place them; just to fix the plants in their due position. When one drill is thus planted, immediately with the rake draw the earth into the drill over the plants; and then open another drill, proceed in the same method till the whole is planted. Then let the surface of the bed be raked smooth, and cleared from stones, &c.

At each corner of every bed, let a firm stake be driven into the ground, to serve as a mark for the alleys.

It is the custom with some people, who are obliged to make the most of every spot of ground, to sow a thin crop of onions, the first year, on new asparagus beds; and this should be performed before the beds are raked; sowing the seeds and raking them lightly in. A crop of onions may thus be obtained, without hurting the asparagus, provided the onions are not suffered to grow just about the plants.

The asparagus being planted, the next care is, when the plants come up, which will be about the end of this month, or the beginning of the next, to keep them clean from weeds; which must be particularly attended to during the summer season.—[For the further management in dressing up the beds, &c. which must be done this month, see October.]

It will be two years, from the time of planting two year old roots, before the asparagus will produce handsome buds large enough for use; tho' sometimes a few of the largest are cut the second spring after planting. But I do advise to let it be the third year before you make a general cutting.

A plantation of asparagus, if the beds are properly dressed every year, as directed, in the spring and autumn months, will continue to produce buds for twelve or fourteen years.

In making new plantations of asparagus, it is the custom with some gardeners, instead of putting in your plants as before directed, to sow the seed at once in the beds, where the plants are to remain: This is not a bad method—for by such practice the roots are not disturbed by a removal, and consequently cannot fail of producing a regular crop. But it must be observed, that if two pieces of ground are to be laid down the same year with asparagus; supposing one piece to be planted with young roots, and the other sown with seed, that piece which was planted will be ready to cut, a year before that sown with seed.

However to such as choose to raise a plantation of asparagus at once from seed, the method is this:

The beds are to be three feet wide, and prepared as before directed for the plants; then mark out two lines lengthways on the beds, and allowing these lines at the distance of sixteen or eighteen inches, dot in a few seeds, covering them about half an inch deep. When the plants have been up some time, you must thin them, leaving only one of the strongest in each place, and carefully clearing them from weeds—

A plantation of asparagus thus raised will produce beds fit to cut the fourth spring after sowing, but they will be very large and fine the fifth year.

This is now the season to sow asparagus seed, to raise plants to make new plantations.

This seed should be sown about the beginning or middle of this month, on beds of rich earth, about four feet wide, Let it be sown in the broad cast, on the surface; and throw up the alleys about fourteen or sixteen inches wide, and three inches deep; let the seed be buried about half an inch in the earth, and let the ground be raked smooth:—the plants will be up in a month, when they must be kept very clean from weeds, by a careful hand, weeding them at different times in the summer.

If the weather be very dry, when the plants come up, it will be proper to refresh them, now and then, with a little water; which will greatly forward them in their growth.

They will be fit to plant out for good next spring, agreeable to the method prescribed.

 ARTICHOKES

Make a general dressing of artichokes, the beginning or middle of this month.

Where the plants have been landed up in the autumn to protect them from frost, let the ground be now levelled down, especially if the plants have begun to shoot tolerably strong; observe, as you proceed in levelling down, to dig and loosen all the earth about the plants; and at the same time, examine the number of shoots or suckers proceeding from each stool or root; and selecting two or three of the strongest to remain on every stool or root, you may then readily get to slip the superabundant shoots off clean from the place whence they arise; minding, as above directed, to leave two good shoots, but never more than three, upon each root or stock; closing again and gently pressing the earth about the roots, and also about the young plants, with your hands.

The shoots that are slipped off will serve to make fresh plantations, where wanted; for artichokes are generally increased by planting the young shoots; and this is the season to do it.

When any new plantations of artichokes are intended, let them be planted so soon in this month as you can procure good plants for that purpose; observing that those slips or suckers slipped off, in spring dressing, from the largest plants, as above directed, are the proper sets to be chosen.

There are two sorts of artichokes, the large globe, and the French green or oval artichoke; but the former is greatly preferable to plant for a general supply, the head being considerably larger, and the eatable parts more thick and fleshy.

They should be planted in an open situation, and in good ground; it may be necessary therefore to spread a quantity of good rotten dung over the piece, and to dig it in.—The sets must be planted, with a dibble, in rows of five feet asunder, and four feet in the row—give them some water immediately after they are planted, to settle the earth about the plants.

The above plantation, if kept clear from weeds, and watered now and then in dry weather, in the beginning of the spring, till they have taken good root, will not fail to yield artichokes in June.

You may in the spring, when your artichokes are dressed, plant a row of drum head cabbage plants between them, or sow radishes, spinage and lettuce; as also, between the rows of your new planted shoots.

A plantation of artichokes will continue to produce good heads six or seven years, and sometimes longer; but it must be observed, that such persons as desire to have a succession of them for two or three months in the summer, should make a new plantation every spring; for the old stocks, which have been planted a year or two, produce heads in May and June; and the slips planted now produce their heads in June and July.

About the latter end of this month, sow the seed of artichokes; for this purpose choose a small piece of good ground, in an open situation; throw it up into a bed, about four feet wide; draw four drills thereon, about nine inches from each other, and half an inch deep; plant the seeds about six inches distant in the row; cover the seed over and rake the other ground smooth. The plants from these seeds will be fit to put out, &c.

 IRISH POTATOES

Irish potatoes may be planted at any time in this month—these roots thrive best in a moderate, light, loose soil; and where it is not wet, if you add dung it will be of great advantage.

For propagating potatoes be careful to procure some good roots; that is, to pick a quantity of the best kind of potatoes, choosing such as are perfectly sound, and of a tolerable large size: These are to be prepared for planting, by cutting or quartering them; that is to say, each root is to be cut into two, three, or more pieces, minding particularly that each piece be furnished with at least one or two good buds, which will be sufficient. Being thus prepared, they are to be planted in rows two feet and a half from each other, and about a foot in the row, and two inches deep.

As to the method of planting, it is frequently performed with a blunt ended dibble; but some plant them as they proceed in digging or plowing the ground, placing them in the trenches or furrows as they go on, and turning the earth from the next trench or furrow over them; and so on to the end.

Others dig or plough the ground; then draw drills with a hoe, about two or three inches deep; and so drop the set into the drills and cover them in.

But where people plant large quantities, the most expeditious way is to plow them in, by placing the potatoes in the furrows; miss two furrows, and plant one; but you must observe, that your ground must be in good order, clean, and free from weeds, &c.

 TURNIPS

Early in this month, sow turnips for a full crop—the best sort to sow now is the early Dutch. But I observe that few people sow turnips at this season; and the reason is, I have heard many say, that they will all go to seed. But the chief cause why they so frequently run to seed is, that it is greatly degenerated, by being sown too often in the same soil; but you will find that when your seed is fresh imported from Europe, not one in ten thousand will run.

Let this seed be sown in an open spot of ground moderately thin, and as even as possible—lay the ground out in beds from six to ten feet wide; and throw up alleys eighteen inches wide; let the earth that is taken out of the alleys be carefully thrown over the beds; and rake the ground as even as possible, standing in the alleys.

The Fruit Garden

 PLUMB AND CHERRY TREES

Prune, plumb and cherry trees, at any time in this month, if not done before. In pruning plumb and cherry trees, either espaliers or standards; observe, that the same bearers remain many years in a fruitful state.—Let only any causual worn out wood, or any irregular crowded branches, and decayed parts be cut out, together with all the superfluous and ill placed young shoots of last summer.—

But it must be observed, where a supply of young bearing wood is wanting in any part of these trees, that some of the best situated shoots of the last summer's growth must be left in every such place; these shoots are not to be shortened, but each must be left at full length, without being reduced at any future pruning, in summer or winter, where there is room for them.

For the shoots, which are now left at full length, and not hereafter shortened, will, in the second or third year after, begin to produce some thick short shoots or spurs, about an inch or more in length; and

44

upon these spurs, and on no other, the fruit of these
trees is produced.

But on the contrary, if the shoots which are left in
to bear were to be shortened, as by many is igno-
rantly practiced, they would not, in that case, produce any such fruit-bearing spurs; but, in the places
where the spurs or blossom-buds will otherwise appear, would send out numbers of strong and altogether useless shoots; with which the trees would
be continually crowded; and not one branch would
be in a condition to bear, so long as you keep shortening them: and the trees thus mismanaged would not
produce one tenth part of the fruit as when treated
in the method above mentioned.—

Therefore be careful to leave the young shoots as
they advance in full length, without reducing them,
unless you should perceive any irregular or superabundant ones which may require to be taken out, in
which case they should be pruned away close to the
mother branches.

This plainly shows, what method is to be taken, in
pruning these trees, to bring them into a condition
to bear; it also plainly shows, that neither the young
shoots nor old branches are, in the general course
of pruning, to be shortened.

But in the course of pruning the above trees, the
branches in general should be well examined with a
curious eye; and if there are any which are old or
worn out, and not furnished with good bearing
spurs, let such as are decayed, or in an unfruitful
state, be taken out, to make room for the more proper

bearing wood and for a supply of young shoots, in a regular manner.

When the old useless wood is cut out, examine the remaining branches, &c. And where these stand too close let some of them be cut away, observing to prune out the most unpromising and irregularly grown, and such as can be best spared; and let no two branches cross each other—and all the summer shoots which are not wanted for a supply of wood, must be now cut away quite close, leaving no spurs but such as are naturally produced.

Let the shoots in general be left at equal distances, at the extremities; and always observe to leave the middle of the tree open, to admit a free circulation of air through the branches.

PEACHES, NECTARINES, AND APRICOTS

If your peaches, nectarines and apricot trees were not pruned in the last months, let it be done in this; the sooner the better. [For the method see January.]

PRUNING OLD STANDARD FRUIT TREES

Standard fruit trees, in the garden or orchard, may be pruned at any time in this month, where necessary: observing to cut from them all dead wood, and decayed worn out branches, that do not promise to bear good fruit, or that croud others.—Also where the trees assume a rambling or irregular growth, and the wood in general is much crowded. Let such be cut away in a regular manner, so that the principal branches may stand clear of each other.

If any old trees be infested with moss, which some-times runs over the branches; let it now be cleared off, if not done before; for it will much injure both trees and fruit.

 VINES

The vines which were not pruned the former month, should be attended to as soon as possible in this,—If the business be delayed much longer, they will be apt to bleed after pruning; which will greatly injure the plants.

 RASBERRIES

If your rasberries were not pruned, dressed, and planted in the last month, let this work be done early in this. [For the method see January.]

 STRAWBERRIES

The plantations of strawberries should be now cleaned, and have the spring dressing.—First pull or cut off any remaining strings or runners from the plants, and clear the beds from weeds, litter &c. then loosen the ground between the plants, and earth them up: this will strengthen them, and make them flower strongly, and produce large well flavoured fruit.

Strawberries may be planted till the middle of this month; but the best season is about the latter end of September, or the beginning of October; for, in such case, they will bear fruit the summer after: indeed those planted now will take root freely; but will not bear any fruit until the next year.—Observing that the proper sets for planting are the young offsets or runners of last summer; such as I advised to be left in May, which must be now procured from these beds of old plants that are in full perfection for bearing, taking them up with good roots, and not disturbing the old stools. Prepare for these plants a piece of good land, if loomy the better, and let some good rotten dung if you can procure it, be dug in. Divide the ground into beds four feet wide, with alleys at least eighteen inches. Plant four rows on each bed, and let them be about ten inches or a foot distant from each other in the row.

 PLANTING FRUIT TREES

Fruit trees, of all sorts, may be planted any time in this month.

Let every kind be planted at proper distances, so that they may have room to grow, without interfering with each other; which, in a few years, is often the case in many gardens and orchards.

Peaches and nectarines should never be planted less than twenty-five feet distant from each other; and if you plant them thirty, it would be a more eligible plan; tho' the distance appears considerable at first, yet, if trees are grafted or budded upon free growing stocks, they will readily fill up that place; and bear much better than if confined, so as to require to be often cut back, and kept within bounds.

Standard apple and pear trees, when planted in an orchard, should be at least thirty feet distant from each other; and if the land is rich and strong, if they had forty it would be the better.

The rule, I advise, to plant standard fruit trees in general is, to allow apple and fruit trees in an orchard, from thirty to forty feet distance, every way; peaches, nectarines and apricots, from twenty-five to thirty feet distance; cherries and plumbs, from eighteen to twenty-five; almonds, quinces and medlars, from sixteen to twenty. Observing, that these are the least distances that should be allowed; but where there is a good scope of ground, you may allow them five, ten, or even twenty feet more room: for in the end, it will prove to be of greater advantage, when the trees arrive at their full growth.

In planting trees of any kind, let care be taken that they are not planted too deep; for that is a more material point than many people imagine.

Open for each tree a hole, wide enough to receive the roots freely, without pressing them against the sides; then, having the trees ready dug up with good spreading roots, which you must take care not to injure in the operation, let the ends of the straggling ones be pruned; and cut off all such as are broken or bruised: then set the tree in the hole, and see that all the roots spread freely as they should do, so as the upper roots be rather over than below the general surface of the ground.—Break the earth well, and throw it in equally about the roots; and in so doing shake the tree gently, that the earth may fall in close between the roots and fibres.

When the earth is all in, tread the surface gently, to fix the tree properly; and lastly raise a small concave hill round the tree.

Support new planted trees with stakes, as soon as they are planted; that they may not be rocked about by the wind, which will greatly retard their taking root.

 FIG TREES

About the middle of this month prune your fig trees.

In the first place observe to cut away or grub up all the suckers at the stock of the trees; which otherwise would require much nourishment to support them, and weaken the mother plants; when this is done you must prune out all dead, decayed and crowded wood; and where any large branch grows in a rambling manner across the others, let it be also taken out.

Where the branches stand too close, so as not to admit a free circulation of air through the tree, let some of these be also cut away.—The keeping the trees thin, and taking away all irregular and old worn out branches, is the only way to have large and well tasted fruit, and also handsome and lasting trees.

The young branches of fig trees must not be shortened, but left at their full length; for by shortening them you will not only cut away the fruit that would have appeared, but also, occasion them to run much to wood, and thereby never to produce half a crop of fruit.

 TRANSPLANT ORANGE TREES, &c.

If the weather be open and mild, about the latter end of this month, you may transplant such orange, lemon and lime trees, as you have an occasion for. —If you plant the orange trees for a hedge, about ten feet will be a good distance; but if intended for an orchard or a grove, twenty feet will not be too much.

N. B. These trees will not thrive well far off from the salt water.

 PRUNE ORANGE TREES, &c.

About the middle of this month, you may, with great safety, venture to prune your orange, lemon and lime trees.

In doing this, observe to cut out all dead and decayed branches from the middle of the trees, and to take all cobwebs, dead leaves, &c. that shall be found on them.

 HEADING DOWN YOUNG TREES

In heading down those trees, it is to be supposed that they were budded or grafted a year or two before, and have been trimmed up to a small head about the

51

height of three or four feet, containing four or five small shoots, and an upright middle one.—Cut the middle one down close, leaving four or five of the shoots; thus done, shorten the remaining ones within six or seven eyes from the main stem, if the tree is in a strong and vigorous state; but if the tree is weak, the shoots may be shortened to three or four eyes: by your shortening the branches as above, it contributes much to the growth of the trees the next summer.

MARCH

Work to be done in the Kitchen Garden

 BEANS

Y OU MAY STILL continue to plant more beans to succeed those sown in the former months, where a constant succession of young ones are required.

The long podded bean is a proper kind to plant at this season, it being a remarkable great bearer, excellent when young, and is very profitable for the use of a family.—They may be planted at any time in this month, allowing them the distance of three feet between each row, and about six inches in the rows.—

The Windsor and Sandwich beans, or any other of the large kinds may yet be planted—let these be planted at this season in rows about five feet asunder.

—Let some earth be drawn up to the stems of such beans as are advanced four or five inches high, which will greatly promote their growth.

 PEAS

Sow peas to succeed those sown in the former month: where a constant supply is required, there should be some sown at least every fortnight or three weeks.

The marrowfat and Spanish morotto, being of the large kind, are both fine eating peas, and great bearers, and are also proper to be sown at this season—likewise, the rouncival is a very fine large pea for a late crop; and if sown at any time this month; will succeed very well. These large kind of peas should be sown in drills or trenches not less than five feet asunder. The hotspur, or any other small peas are also proper to be sown now, if required.

Draw earth to such peas as are come up, and advanced to the height of two or three inches; it will strengthen the plants, and greatly forward their growth.

Set sticks to peas when you intend them for to climb up; this should be done in due time, when the plants are about four or five inches high; observe to have sticks of a proper heighth: for marrowfats and other large peas, they should be six or seven feet high; but those of four or five feet will be quite sufficient for the hotspurs, and other sorts of small peas.

MARCH

 CABBAGES

Now transplant, if not done in February, all the cabbage plants that are remaining in their winter beds, or as many as you intend to plant out for a spring crop: this should be done the beginning of the month; and if the weather proves dry, give your plants now and then a little water till they have taken good root.

Draw up earth about the stems of forward cabbage plants, as it will greatly strengthen them and encourage their growth.

If the weather about this time should prove dry, you should frequently give your young cabbage plants a little water, observing to do it early in the morning.

 SNAP OR BUSH BEANS

About the latter end of this month, plant snap beans, in a dry and warm situation.

The best sorts to plant for a first crop are the small negro, and also the white and yellow dwarfs; they are exceeding good bearers, and will come very early.

These beans should be planted in rows, about two feet from each other, and, at this season, about three inches distant from each other in the rows.

 ONIONS AND LEEKS

Where onions and leeks were not sown the last month, this work should be done early in this.—You may either sow them in the broad cast, or in trenches, about nine or ten inches from each other, on beds about four feet wide.

The onions and leeks sown last month will be now above the ground; let them be hoed as soon as you can properly distinguish the rows:—for nothing will promote the growth of onions and leeks so much as frequent hoeings.

Let your transplanted onions be often hoed, and the earth kept always loose between them; which will greatly promote their growth.

 TURNIPS

If you have not yet sown any turnips, let this business be no longer delayed.—[For the method see February.]

Those turnips which were sown the beginning of last month, should be now hoed, and properly thinned, leaving the strongest plants from six to eight inches distant from each other; but if they were sown in drills nine or ten inches apart, they should be also thinned to about six or eight.—[For particulars of hoeing turnips see August.]

 IRISH POTATOES

Potatoes may be yet planted, but the sooner the better—plant them about two feet and half asunder.

Those planted in the beginning of last month, will be now above the ground; they should have some earth drawn up close to them—it will protect them from the frost, and cold winds, and greatly promote their growth.

 CARROTS AND PARSNIPS

If you have not sowed any carrots or parsnips last month, let some be sown the beginning of this.

If you do not sow at this season the true orange carrot, the greatest part will run to seed before they arrive to any degree of perfection: but if you can procure good seed imported from Europe, and if your land is good, and you follow the directions of last month, you need not fear of having a fine crop of carrots and parsnips.:—However, where a supply of young carrots or parsnips are required, they ought to be sown almost every month.

 RADISHES

Thin the general crops of radishes where they are too thick—you may begin to draw them before they become quite so large as a goose quill, which will make room for the other plants to grow more freely; observe to keep the crop clear from weeds.

Radish seed, both the short top and salmon, should be sown at two different times in this month; by which means a constant supply of young radishes may be obtained; allowing about fifteen or sixteen days between each sowing; choosing at this time, an open situation for your seed;—sow it evenly on the surface, and rake it well in; the plants will make their appearance in a few days, at this season.

The crops of early radishes should in dry weather be frequently watered; this will occasion their swelling freely, and prevent their growing hot and sticky.

Where turnip-rooted radishes, or small round radishes are required, the seed may be sown at any time in this month.—It should be sown in an open spot; and when the plants begin to shew their rough leaves, if they are too thick, they should be thinned to about an inch distance, to make room for the remaining plants to grow.

The black and white Spanish radish may also be sown at any time in this month.

 LETTUCES

About the beginning, or at any time in this month, transplant lettuces of all kinds, where they stand too close; both those of the winter standing, and such as were sown in January, or early in last month.

Choose a good spot of ground for these plants; and if moderately dunged, it will prove beneficial to their growth: dig the ground regularly one spade deep, and rake the surface smooth; then plant the lettuces on beds, about four or four feet and a half wide, divide the beds into four rows, and place your plants about 12 inches from each other in the rows: if the weather be dry, water them immediately after planting; and frequently repeat it till they have taken good root.

MARCH

Coss, cabbage, Silesia, and brown Dutch lettuce, or any other sort may be sown at any time in this month—dig a spot of rich ground for them, in an open situation; sow the seed equally, but not too thick; rake it in lightly: repeat the sowing once a fortnight or three weeks, that there may be a regular succession.

 SMALL SALLADING

Sow small sallading at least once a fortnight, such as mustard, cresses, rape, &c.

Draw some flat shallow drills for these seeds, where the ground is rich and light; sow thereon each kind separate, and cover them lightly with earth.

Water them moderately, if the weather be dry; as it will greatly promote their growth.

If the sallading be attacked with a hoary morning frost, water it off before the sun comes on it; as it will prevent its becoming black and being spotted.

 PARSLEY

If you sowed no parsley seed in the last month, do it early in this; the curled sort is best esteemed, it being most proper to garnish dishes, and equally fit for the kitchen service.

 TOMATOES

About the middle, or towards the latter end of this month, sow tomatoes.

This seed should be sown at this season in a warm situation, and in a light rich soil; it may be sown either in drills, or in the broad cast, or else dotted into the earth about three or four inches asunder, and a quarter of an inch deep.

 SOW PEPPERS OF ALL SORTS

Towards the twentieth of this month, you may sow peppers of different kinds; they may be sown much in the same manner as the tomatoes, and in a warm border of light rich earth.

 WATER AND MUSK MELONS

About the middle of this month, you may sow water and musk melons, for the first crop; the culture of these is so well known, that it needs but little description. I would only recommend it to those who plant melons at this season, to raise hills of good light rich earth, from eight inches to a foot above the surface of the ground; and let the hills be from fourteen to eighteen inches broad on the top, and let about six or seven seeds be placed in each, about half an inch deep.

 CUCUMBERS

Sow cucumbers, for a first crop, about the middle of this month; chuse a warm and sheltered situation, raising hills and managing them in every respect as you would do your melons.—[For the further method of raising them see April.]

 OCRA

Ocra may also be sown about the middle of this month; it delights in a low, rich land; and should be sown in rows, about six feet asunder, and the plants should be left to remain in the rows at least four feet distant.

 SQUASHES AND PUMPKINS

These may be planted about the middle of this month, for the first crop; if they succeed, they will come in early.—[For the method see next month.]

 RED BEETS

The beets that were sown in the last month should be now carefully thinned, leaving only one plant in the place where they were sown, and let the earth be constantly kept loose; which will greatly strengthen the plants.

Red beets ought by no means to be transplanted; for, if the tap root is once broken, it will put out many fibres, and will be very short and unseemly.

 CELERY

About the middle of this month, sow celery for a first crop—prepare a spot of rich ground for this purpose, and as much in the shade as possible, but not under trees; and if it be moist it is all the better.—Sow the seed pretty thick, and either rake it in lightly, or otherwise cover it over near a quarter of an inch with fine earth; and, in dry weather, give frequent moderate waterings, both before and after the seed comes up.

 SPINAGE

Sow spinage where required, it will yet succeed, and may be sown any time in this month.—Where a constant supply of this plant is wanted, you should sow some at least every three weeks; observing the round leafed is still the best sort for this season, which may be sown either in the broad cast and raked in, or in shallow drills.

Hoe the spinage that was sown in the former month, and thin the plants out to three or four inches distance.

 ASPARAGUS

Fork or dress your asparagus beds, if not yet done; let these be finished the first week in this month, for the buds are now in great forwardness.—Rake the bed smooth immediately after they are forked.

Asparagus may yet be planted, it will now take root freely; but let this work be finished by the middle of the month, for the plants will not succeed well if planted later.—Let the same method be observed as mentioned in the former months.

MARCH

Sow Asparagus seed, if omitted last month, in order to raise plants for a new plantation the next year, if required.

 ARTICHOKES

Where artichokes were not dressed and slipped last month, they should be now attended to; for they will have made their spring shoots, which will be up some height above the ground; let the same method be observed in dressing them as directed in February.

Plant artichokes where wanted: they will yet succeed; and may bear in the summer, provided you plant them soon in this month.

Choose a piece of good ground for these plants, in an open situation, and lay some good rotten dung thereon and dig it in a proper depth—let the plants be set in rows five feet asunder, and plant them not less than five feet in the rows, giving them a good watering.

The Fruit Garden

 ORANGE TREES, &c.

About the beginning of this month, you may with great safety transplant orange, lemon, and lime trees. You must also observe to prune them if not done before. [See Feb.]

63

 FIG TREES

About the beginning of this month plant fig trees, if not done in February; this being a good season for removing them—they will now take root in a short time.

These trees should be planted, from twenty to twenty five feet from each other; for nothing adds more to the flavor of the fruit than a free circulation of air and the admission of the sun between the trees and branches.

When you plant them examine the plants well; and rub off all the buds that are likely to break within two feet of the ground; and in particular under the surface of the earth—for they are very apt to throw out suckers, which, if not taken away in due time, will greatly retard the growth of the young trees.

PEACH, NECTARINE, AND APRICOT TREES

Where peach, nectarine, and apricot trees remain unpruned, let them be finished the first week in this month at the furthest—for, if the spring is forward, these trees are sometimes in full bloom at this time; when it will do them more hurt than good to prune them in such state—and the work might have been much better done in the former months.

In pruning these trees, let the same methods be observed as directed in February; but as the buds are now swelled it will require the greater caution.

Finish pruning of apples, pears, plumbs, and cherries, and all other fruit trees; it should not at any rate be delayed longer than the first week in this month.

PLANTING FRUIT TREES

If you have been hitherto dilatory, fruit trees may yet be planted with some hopes of success, but the sooner the better; if the weather be moist, the trees which are planted now will take root in a short time, and, with the assistance of a little water in dry weather, will shoot freely.

In planting fruit trees, either espaliers or standards, observe to plant each kind at the distances mentioned under the head in the month of February.

STRAWBERRIES

The strawberry beds, which were not dressed in the last month, ought to be attended to as soon as possible in this; the plants will now begin to push apace, and the sooner this work is done the better.

Clear the beds from weeds, and the plants from strings, and other litter, and if the main plants are crouded with young ones, from last year's runners, let them be thinned accordingly; for it is the best method to keep those plants in single bunches, and clear of each other, so that there may be room to dig round them with a narrow spade or trowel.—The beds being cleared from litter, &c. loosen the earth between the plants, and let rich earth, or well rotted dung be put in between them; as it will be the means of strengthening the plants, and cause them to flower strong, and produce large and good fruit.

Strawberries may now be planted, where required —observe the same method as mentioned in October.

It seems to be a common method in Carolina to burn the dead leaves, and runners of strawberries in the spring; I am much against such practice; for by burning the dead leaves and runners, you often injure the plants likewise.

APRIL

Work to be done in the Kitchen Garden

 BEANS

IN THE COUNTRY, you may yet venture to plant beans the beginning of this month, for the last crop.

The Windsor and the long podded beans are the best sort to plant at this season; the former should be planted in rows about four feet distant from each other, and six or eight inches in the row; and the latter, about three feet, and five or six inches from each other in the rows.

Hoe between the rows of beans that are already up, and draw earth about their stems.

Observe to top such beans as are in full blossom;

it will promote the setting of the pods. [See February.]

 PEAS

Sow some peas, in order to have a regular supply from the beginning of this month; let this be your last crop; indeed there is no great prospect of success even from this; but where young peas are required, and you have plenty of garden room in the country, you may try to get some peas to come in for use about June; tho' it is seldom you see any in Charleston market after May that are good.

The best sort to sow at this season is the marrowfat, green and white rouncevil, being fine large sorts; likewise any of the hotspur kinds may be sown now, and will sometimes produce a good crop.

The larger kinds ought to be planted five feet from row to row, and the hotspur four feet at least.

Let the earth be now drawn up to the stems of such peas as are above ground, and keep them clear from weeds; for by this means their growth will be greatly promoted.

Stick such peas as are advanced to the height of five inches; let it not be delayed too long, for if they are once beat down by the winds and rain, it will be troublesome to stick them at all, and they will not readily rise again.

Let hotspurs have sticks about three feet and a half, or four feet high; and larger sorts sticks of about six feet.

APRIL

 CABBAGES

By the beginning of this month your spring sown cabbage plants will be fit to remove to the beds where you intend them to cabbage.

Plant out the early York and sugar loaf, for they will be the first that will produce hard heads: they should be also the first made use of, as they will not stand the heat so well as the larger kind of cabbages.

These plants should be planted in a square of well dunged land, at about two feet from row to row, and two feet from each other in the row.

Next plant the battersea and drumhead cabbages; allow them two feet and a half from row to row, and two feet in the row.

Let the cabbage plants, which were set out in February and March, have frequent hoeings, and draw up earth to the stems of them.

About the middle, or latter end of this month, sow large late cabbages and savoys for a general autumn crop.—These seeds should be sown in an open and airy situation, in beds about four feet wide; the seed ought not to be sown very thick, nor yet too thin, but moderately and evenly scattered.

The plants which are sown now will be fit to plant out in June.

 CAULIFLOWERS AND BROCOLI

Sow your first crop of cauliflowers and brocoli, at the same time, and much in the same manner as you do cabbage plants. If you sow them early, they will be able to stand the sun in the summer much better than those sown in June.

 SNAP OR BUSH BEANS

Now plant full crops of all kinds of snap and bush beans, to succeed those sown in the last month.

Any of the dwarf kind may be now planted; but the most profitable are the white, black, and yellow, which are all early kinds, great bearers, and exceeding good for kitchen use.

There are three or four other kinds more late, but very great bearers; they are the black speckled, red speckled, large white, and the cream coloured dwarfs. The early and the late sorts may be planted at the same time in this month, and they will succeed each other in bearing.

The method of planting them is this.—Dig a square of ground, in an open situation; and if you can give it a moderate dunging, the better.

Your ground being dug, rake it even; and take away the stones if any; then with a small hoe draw drills about twenty inches or two feet from each other, and one inch deep; then drop the beans into the bottom of the drills six inches apart; cover them over with your hoe, and rake the ground smooth.

Let it be observed, that both the early and late sorts are to be planted in the same manner; only allow the large kinds a little more room from row to row, and likewise in the rows.

70

The white running snap bean is in the highest esteem in Europe; where few families use dwarfs after these come in.—They are great bearers, and a fine delicious vegetable if gathered while young. I have known them to thrive exceeding well in this state, and am much surprized to see them taken so little notice of; for they will bear when the dwarfs will not—I have seen them in full bearing in July and August.

These beans should be planted in rows about six feet from each other, and from four to six inches in the rows, and in drills about an inch deep, as was before observed.

 CARROTS AND PARSNIPS

Your early carrots and parsnips will be now advancing fast in their growth, and they should be properly encouraged:—Clear them from weeds, and thin the plants out to their due distances.

This work may be either done with the hand or hoe; but those who can use the small hoe will find it to be the most expeditious method of cleaning and thining the plants: and besides, by loosening the ground with the hoe, it will in a great manner promote their growth.

However, at any rate, let the plants be thined out properly, so that they may have full liberty to grow at the top, and to swell at the bottom. Thin out therefore the general crops to about seven or eight inches at least, and cut up all the weeds, for there is nothing like allowing these plants plenty of room; by which means, if the ground be good, the roots will become long and strait.

The parsnips in particular should be thined out to twelve inches distance; then the roots will swell to a considerable size, and attain their utmost perfection.

Such crops of carrots however, as are intended to be drawn for the table when young, need not to be thined at first, to more than four or five inches apart; for, by the gradual thining out the larger, for use, the rest will increase in their growth daily.

But the main crops of carrots, that you intend to grow to a full size, should be thined properly at once; you should in this case allow them full eight or nine inches at least; but if they were placed from ten to twelve inches asunder, it would be the better.

 SOWING CARROTS AND PARSNIPS

About the latter end of this month, sow carrots and parsnips for a general winter crop.

Various are the opinions about sowing these roots for winter use; therefore I think it incumbent on me to let no observation escape that may add to the culture of these valuable vegetables.

In England the culture of carrots has arrived to such perfection, that for my own credit I refrain from relating real facts; for I am sure, not one in a thousand would believe me.

It seems to be the general opinion of most people,

that if they sow their winter crops of carrots before June, they will run all to seed; but those ideas are entirely erroneous; for success depends chiefly on the kind of seed.—If it be the true orange carrot, it will not run;—but if the seed sown in March or April, be of the pale degenerated sort, they will run to seed by September; or, as the gardeners express it, they will all be speared to a plant; while the produce of the true genuine seed imported from Europe, will be in its full vigor. Besides, it is a very hard matter to get the carrot seed to grow in June, that month often proving dry, and the weather very hot; therefore people who have occasion to sow large crops of carrots for the winter use, should take every precaution to keep the ground as dry as possible.

Let it be laid out in beds about four feet or four feet and half wide; observing to lay the beds always on the descent, and not to confine the alleys, but let them be full fifteen inches wide, and not less than six inches deep; by which means you will be able to draw off the water; for if it is suffered to lay on the beds or even in the alleys, the intense heat of the sun in July and August, will scald the roots and rot them.

Having laid out the ground into beds, let the surface be raked smooth; then draw four drills on each bed at equal distances, about half an inch deep; and scatter the seeds thin in each drill; cover the seed with your hoe; and rake the ground even standing in the alleys.

 ONIONS AND LEEKS

The onions that were transplanted in the autumn will now begin to swell, and many of them will begin to put forth seed heads;—let those be pulled out as soon as they appear; for if they are suffered to stay long on the plants they will not only deform the roots, but will also draw from them great part of the nourishment; therefore let them be taken out as soon as they appear.

The onions sown in February will be now advancing fast in their growth; let them be thined out to their proper distances; and leave them in the row about eight inches from each other, and loosen the ground between and round the plants, which will greatly forward the growth both of onions and leeks.

 SOWING LEEKS

About the latter end of this month sow leeks for winter use.

These may be sown in a small bed of good earth, pretty thick, from whence you may transplant them as soon as they are fit.

TURNIPS

Hoe and thin the turnips that were sown in the last months; cut up all the weeds and thin the plants regularly; allow eight or nine inches between plant and plant; if sown broad cast.

This work of thining should always be performed when the rough leaves are about the size of a shilling.

 ASPARAGUS

Asparagus, you will be now cutting for use; in cutting the buds, or shoots of these plants, it should be observed that, when they are arrived to about three or four inches in height they should be gathered.— But if these five or six inches high, or in prime order, when permitted to run any higher, the top of the bud opens, and the shoot does not eat so well as those that are cut when the head is quite close.

When you cut them, be careful to thrust your knife down close by the side of the shoot you intend to cut, least you wound, or destroy any of the buds that are coming up, and do not yet appear, cutting the young shoots off about three or four inches under the ground.

Let the beds of these plants be now cleared of weeds, which will come up very thick among them.

Taking therefore an opportunity of a dry day, and with a small hoe cut up all the weeds clean within the surface, and they will soon die.

 IRISH POTATOES

Potatoes will be now coming forward, and should frequently be hoed, which will keep them clean of weeds.

Continue still to draw more earth up to the stems

of your potatoes, which will be of great service to them.

 RADISHES

Sow more radishes; the salmon kind is very proper for this sowing; and likewise the short top and turnip. —Choose an open situation for sowing these seeds; and let your ground be dug well, and divided into beds about four feet wide; sow the seeds (but not too thick at this season) cast a little earth over the beds, and rake the surface even, standing in the alleys.

It will be proper to sow radishes at two or three different times in this month, to continue a succession.

In dry weather let your radishes be frequently watered both before and after they are up, which will prevent their growing hot and sticky.

 LETTUCES

In moist weather transplant lettuces of various kinds, that were sown in the last month.

Choose a rich spot of land for these plants, in a free and open situation; such as is not crowded with trees, &c. which will draw the plants up slender, without forming good heads.

Dig the ground neatly, and throw it up into beds about four feet wide; rake the surface smooth, and plant four rows on each bed, about nine inches from each other in the rows.

If the weather be dry, give them frequently a little water till they have taken good root.

Sow lettuce this month, to succeed the last month's sowing; and where a constant supply of lettuce is required, this should be sown at least twice in April.

The best kinds to sow now are, the Silesia, cabbage, and brown Dutch: the coss lettuces are very apt when sown at this season to run to seed before they arrive to any degree of perfection.

Sow these seeds in an open situation, very thin, for it is designed that they should remain where they were sown, till they are fit for use. Let it be observed, that they will not run to seed as soon as if they were to be transplanted, and will make much larger and finer heads.

Let those seeds be sown in beds about four feet wide, and throw up good bold alleys; and you may also sow a sprinkling of radishes amongst the lettuce; observe not to sow them too thick.

If the weather prove dry let the seed be watered both before and after they are up.

 SMALL SALLADING

You may still continue to sow mustard, cresses, radish, rape, &c. if they are required.

Where a constant supply of these small herbs are wanted, there should be some sown every week.

 CELERY

About the beginning, or at any time in this month, you may sow celery for a general crop.

Dig a small piece of light, rich earth, and lay the surface even, and throw it up into beds; then sow the seeds pretty thick, and rake it as light as possible, with an even hand.

If the weather should prove dry, let the seeds have a little water both before and after they are come up.

 MINT

Mint may be also planted now, where new beds are wanted.

The sets proper for this purpose are, the young plants which come up from the old ones, as observed in the former months—they should be planted in a spot of rich ground, after being dug, and divided into beds about four feet wide, and set five rows of plants on each bed, about eight inches from each other in the rows, and give them a good watering to settle the earth about their roots.

 CUCUMBERS AND MELLONS

Sow cucumbers and melons, about the beginning of this month, for a full crop. For this purpose, choose a piece of good ground in a sheltered situation; and if you can procure any good rotten dung, put about half a wheel-barrow full to each hill, and cover it over with rich earth, about six inches deep, and plant thereon about six or seven seeds.

 SQUASHES AND PUMKINS

Sow also, about the beginning of this month, squashes and pumkins; for there is now a fair prospect of their succeeding: let them be sown or planted in the same manner as cucumbers, &c.

 OKRA

At any time in this month, you may sow or plant okra seeds: but, if you have not planted any before now, the sooner they are put into the ground the better.

Those seeds should be sown, or planted on ridges or hills, on low ground, about four or five feet from each other, and three or four feet apart in the rows.

 THINING BEETS

The beets that were sown in February, will require thining early in this month, if not done before.

Let all the small plants be taken away, and leave the strong ones about a foot from each other, in the rows—then, with a hoe loosen the earth between them, and about the plants that remain; which will greatly forward their growth.

 DESTROY WEEDS

Weeds will now begin to appear plentifully from seeds, in every part of the garden; and the utmost diligence should be used to destroy them while young, before they get a head of the crops.

Pay particular regard to your onions, carrots, parsnips, lettuce, spinage, and the like; for the weeds grow much quicker than they do; and if they are not weeded, or hoed in time, the weeds will soon over top the plants, and occasion much trouble to clear them.

Those who are expert in using the small hoe, where seeds are sown, either broad cast or in drills, will dispatch more work in one day, than six will do at hand weeding in the same time.

Take the opportunity of dry weather, and hoe ground between the beans, pease, cabbages, and other crops that stand wide, to destroy the weeds, and take care to tread the ground as little as possible.

A large piece of ground may soon be got over with a hoe, when the weeds are small; but when they are permitted to grow large, it requires much labour to destroy them.

Fruit Garden

 VINES

Vines should be looked over about the middle of this month—they will by this time have made some shoots; and the useless ones should be displaced.

In looking over vines, observe, at this time to displace only such shoots as appear absolutely useless. —There generally arises many young shoots from the old wood, and younger branches; but these seldom produce grapes, or wood proper to bear fruit: therefore, let most of these shoots be rubbed off close, except in such places where young wood will be wanted next year, which should be strictly attended to; and leave for the present, all the shoots that are produced from the last year's wood.

But where two shoots put out from one eye, which often happens, let the most unlikely be taken away; for if they were both suffered to remain, one would starve the other, and the fruit of neither will be good.

Let it be observed, that this dressing, or displacing of useless shoots, at this early time, may be performed with the finger and thumb, rubbing them off quite close.

The useless shoots being cleared away, the useful ones when of due length, should be trained along the frame, so that each may enjoy the advantage of the sun and air, to promote its growth, together with that of the fruit.

By the above early regulating the grape vines, the bunches of grapes will be large and fine, and will ripen more regularly and sooner then when the vines are suffered to run into confusion before they are looked over;—besides by timely looking over the vines, one may do as much work in one hour, as in six, when the shoots are suffered to run and mix in a confused and irregular manner.

 STRAWBERRY BEDS

Both the old and new beds of strawberries, should be kept free from weeds; and the runners produced from these plants, should be constantly taken off as they come forth; but where new plantations of straw-berries are required, some of the best runners may be suffered to remain till September, to form young plants—observe always, to stop the runners soon after forming the first plants; and these are to be planted out in the autumn as there directed.

About the beginning of this month, let the straw-berry beds now in fruit, be frequently watered in dry weather, for they will require it. If they are not well supplied with water in a dry time, the fruit will be small and ill tasted, and there will be also but a thin crop.

APRIL

 WATERING NEW PLANTED TREES

New planted trees, both standards and dwarfs, should, in dry weather, be well watered at the roots about once a week—it will also be of service to water the branches now and then in dry weather, which frequently happens in this and the two following months.

MAY

Work to be done in the Kitchen Garden

 SNAP BEANS

S NAP BEANS may be planted at any time in this month; but to have a constant supply they ought to be planted every week.

Choose a piece of good ground in an open situation for them at this season; and if the ground is dry, you may soak the seed about six or eight hours in soft water before you plant them.

Having dug your ground, proceed to draw drills, as advised in the former month; then drop the beans in the drills or trenches, about five or six inches distant from each other; cover them up with your hoe, and rake the ground smooth.—[For further information see last month.]

84

MAY

Let some earth be now drawn up to the stem of such snap or bush beans as require it; which will strengthen them greatly.

 CABBAGES AND SAVOYS

If your general crop of cabbage plants, for the autumn and winter use, were not sown last month, let them be sown early in this, that they may have time to get strength before the hot weather comes in: for I find, by experience, that people in general seldom sow their cabbage plants before June, and often not till July.—If they are not sown before June, the seeds frequently lie in the ground till the sun destroys them; for June commonly proves the dryest month in the year; and we have often very heavy rains in July that cripple the plants before they get strength.— These and a number of other reasons may be added in favor of April and May, for sowing winter cabbages.

Let your cabbage plants, which are put out, have frequent hoeings; and draw earth to the stems of those that require it.

 CAULIFLOWERS AND BROCOLI

About the beginning or the middle of this month, if not sown in the last, sow your cauliflower and brocoli seed, for a full crop.

Prepare a small piece of land in an open situation for these seeds; dig the ground, and lay it even; throw it up into beds, and sow your seeds, but not too thick; and cover them over with a little earth, and rake the ground smooth, for it is proposed, that these plants should grow to a good size before they are put out for good.

 CARROTS AND PARSNIPS

If your general crop of carrots and parsnips for autumn and winter use, were not sown last month, let them be sown early in this, the sooner the better; for if they are sown the latter end of the month, when the dry weather generally sets in, you must be constantly watering the ground to get them up, and they will acquire but little strength before the hot weather comes on, and are liable to be scalded after every mid-day's shower of rain.—[For the work see April.]

 LETTUCES

Sow Silesia, brown Dutch, and cabbage lettuce.

Sow the seed in this season where they are to stand for use, in the most low and shady part of the garden, but not under trees.

It is of little use to transplant lettuces at any time in this month; for by so doing they will run to seed, and arrive to no degree of perfection.

 SMALL SALLADING

Sow small sallading at least once a week; such as mustard, cress, rape, &c.—Draw some drills about four

86

inches from each other, and sow the seeds pretty thick, and throw a little earth over them; rake it smooth, and let the ground be watered as soon as the seeds are sown, if the weather be dry.

 RADISHES

Sow salmon and turnip radishes, at any time in this month; and where a constant supply of these roots are required, the seed should be sown once a week or fortnight.—Sow it at this season, in an open situation, and not too thick; for the tops of the salmon radishes in this month, will grow to a large size before the roots are fit to draw.—A small sprinkling of lettuce may be sown with the radishes; for when the latter comes off, the former will succeed them.

 SPINAGE

You may yet continue to sow spinage seed, where required.

Prepare a piece of good ground in an open situation; and throw it up into beds about four feet wide: you may either sow the spinage seed in broad cast, or in drills; and were you to sow a sprinkling of radishes with the spinage, it would not be amiss.

 CELERY

You may sow more celery about the ginning of this month, for a late crop.

Choose a small piece of low ground, in a shady situation, for sowing this seed now;—let it be sown pretty thick; and water it in dry weather before and after it comes up.

The celery plants that were sown in March, will be fit to prick out towards the middle of this month, into a nursery bed of light, rich earth.

For this purpose, prepare a spot of good ground, and divide it into beds about three or four feet wide; rake the surface smooth; then thin out a quantity of the best plants from the seed bed, and let them be planted on these, about three inches separate from each other; give them a moderate watering, and repeat it every day in dry weather, till they have taken good root.

The plants should remain in these beds till the middle of July; when they may be planted out for good, in trenches.

 CUCUMBERS, MELONS, SQUASHES, &c.

At any time in this month, you may sow a successional crop of cucumbers, melons, squashes, &c.

The seeds at this season, should be sown in an open situation; and if the weather proves dry, give them a little water before they come up; and the plants should be frequently watered in dry weather, after they are up.

MAY

 PEPPERS AND TOMATOES

The peppers and tomatoes that were sown the beginning of last month, will be by the middle of this, fit to plant out, where they are to stand for good.

For this purpose, choose a piece of good ground in a free and open situation; draw the earth up in a small ridge, and plant the peppers in rows about two feet from each other, and from twelve to eighteen inches in the rows.

The tomatoes should be planted in hills about five feet from each other, and three plants on each hill.

 BEETS

If your beets for winter use, were not sown in last month, let it be done early in this; that they may get strength before the hot weather comes in.—[For the method see February.]

 GATHER SWEET AND POT HERBS

Towards the later end of this month, gather mint, balm, sage, thyme, hysop, savory, &c. for drying: provided the plants are nearly at their full growth.

Gather also all such physical herbs as are now in flower.

The latter should be always gathered when they begin to flower; for they are then in their greatest perfection, and much the best for their several pur-

poses; nor should they be gathered before that period.

They must be cut in a dry day, and immediately
spread or hung up in a dry room, out of the reach of
the sun, where they may dry gently—Never lay
those herbs in the sun to dry, for that would exhaust
them too much, and render them useless.

CUT PEPPER-MINT, &c. FOR DISTILLING

These and other plants that are intended to be dis-
tilled, should be gathered for that purpose when they
arrive almost to their full growth, and begin to flower, as before observed; therefore if they do not begin
to flower this month, defer cutting them till the next.

But be sure to cut them in a fine day, and when the
plants are perfectly dry.

DESTROYING WEEDS

Now let more than common pains be taken to destroy weeds among crops of every kind, and in every
part throughout the garden.

There is no work in the kitchen garden that requires more attention than this: for weeds are at no
time more dangerous to crops than at the present: it
should be therefore the principal care of the gardener
to destroy them before they grow large; for weeds,
when permitted to get to much size, not only exhaust
the goodness of the land, and ruin the present crops,

but are also a very disagreeable sight, and require more than double labour to clear the ground of them.

Let the utmost attention be paid to your small crops that grow pretty close; and let them be timely cleared.

That is, let the weeds be cleared away and not suffered to over-spread the plants, which they would soon do when they begin to run, and in this case would do much damage to the crops.

Besides, when the weeds are suffered to grow large among the small crops, so as to mix and entangle one with another, and with the plants, it renders the work of hoeing or weeding them extremely tedious, and very troublesome to perform.

But when weeds appear between the rows of beans, pease, cabbages, and such crops as stand in wide rows, nothing can be more easy than to stop their progress; because, there is room between the plants to admit a large hoe—and with such an instrument a person may go over a large piece of ground in a little time; therefore he who would suffer weeds to grow among such crops will be much to blame.

 WATERING NEW PLANTED CROPS

Watering, in dry weather, is now a very needful work, to all new transplanted crops; always apply it to such as are conveniently situated; and where the number of plants are not too great, so as to render the work over laborious and tedious; repeat the watering till the plants have taken good root.—A regular attention to this business will prove very beneficial, in accelerating the fresh rooting, and setting the plants off in a free growth from the beginning, which would otherwise be greatly checked or stinted.

Fruit Garden

THINNING PEACHES, NECTARINES, AND APRICOTS

These trees, in favourable seasons, will set ten times as much fruit as their roots are capable of supplying with proper nourishment; and if the whole, or even too many of them were to be left, they would starve one another; and the fruit in general would be small and ill flavoured.

Besides, where this precaution is not observed and too great a quantity of these sorts of fruit remain to ripen on the trees, the ill consequence does not terminate altogether in the badness of the fruit that year, but it extends to two or three years to come.—For by suffering the trees to be over burdened with fruit, the branches are robbed of their due nourishment; and the trees are so much exhausted that they will not be able to produce shoots capable of bearing fruit the next, and perhaps subsequent year;—and it may probably be the third year before a crop of good fruit can be reasonably expected.

Therefore when the fruit is produced too thick upon the trees, and advanced to about the size of a nutmeg, or before; let the quantity be reduced;—and the sooner the work is done the better it is for the trees, and also for the fruit that is to remain on them.

This thinning should be performed in a very careful manner, by looking over the branches regularly one by one; and, before you take any off, single out, on each shoot, the fruit that is proper to leave, and let the most promising and best shapen remain:— paying a due regard to those that are best situated on the branches:—each kind according to its size must be left at such proper distances, that every one may have sufficient room to swell and grow freely to its just bigness every way; and the fruit on the strong shoots should be left at least nine or ten inches from each other.—For instance allowing a tree is in good condition and strength for bearing;—and supposing the shoots to be of three different sizes; that is, the strong, the middling, and the weak: the number of fruit to be on those branches are; upon the stronger, three or four of the fairest and best placed; upon the middling shoots two or three, and not more than one on the weak shoots.

Was a due regard to be paid to the above distances, and to the number of fruit mentioned to be left on the different branches; the thinning them nicely in this manner, will be the means of bringing your fruit to the utmost perfection.—At the same time the trees will shoot freely, and produce a sufficient quantity of good wood to bear fruit the next year.

This should be the method of thinning the choice kinds of fruits; but the small and inferior sorts, may be left closer together, and a greater number of fruit may remain upon the different branches:—For instance, the early masculine apricot, the nutmeg peach, and the fair Child's early nectarine are of the earliest kinds, and by far the smallest; of these there may be left upon each of the strong shoots, about five fruit; and on the middle size three or four, and so in proportion on the weaker shoots.

SUMMER PRUNING PEACH, NECTARINE AND APRICOT TREES

About the beginning of this month, you may look over your peach, nectarine and apricot trees—for they will now require your utmost care and attention.

Let these be gone over as quick as possible, while they are making their first shoots, and clear away all the useless ones; and at the same time let the well placed and promising shoots be retained.

Likewise let all the luxuriant shoots that generally rise out of the old wood be taken away;—these will neither produce good fruit nor kindly wood, and will also greatly injure the growth of the prime shoots; they are always known by their rambling and vigorous growth: and as I before observed, in treating of pruning in a former month, branches shooting out from the middle part of the tree should be all displaced, unless any should seem necessary in particular parts, to fill up a vacancy, or to furnish a supply of wood—but only some occasional shoots of these kinds should be left, and let all the others be cleared away quite close.

Notwithstanding, be careful to leave a full sufficiency of the best shoots, that are of a kind and moderate growth; that is, the shoots that are produced this summer, to bear fruit next year; therefore it is much the best way to reserve at this season a sufficient quantity of kindly growing shoots, that there may be enough to choose from in winter pruning.

Observe not to shorten any of the shoots thus left at this season; but let them remain at full length; for by topping them they will produce so many young shoots, as would crowd the fruit too much.

In the early summer dressing or pruning of these kinds of trees, it is also requisite to keep the middle part open to admit a free circulation of air among the branches; which will be very beneficial to the fruit; but, at the same time, not to cut away too much, so as to leave the fruit altogether exposed to the sun.

The displacing of these young shoots at this season may be carefully performed with the finger and thumb; and the fruit may be thinned at the same time as before directed.

 VINES

The vines will now begin to shoot vigorously; and will produce a great number of shoots, many of which will be useless, and must now be cut away; and the sooner the better.

This work should be done before the shoots begin to entangle with each other;—for a great advantage attends this early dressing; both in giving an opportunity of performing the work with more expedition and regularity, and in affording a greater benefit to the trees and fruit.—Observe that all the immediate bearing shoots, which now discover the young bunches of grapes upon them, must be left,—and such other shoots as have strength, and are well situated for the purpose of throwing out bearers next year, must be left in the places where they are wanted; but all weak and straggling shoots, such particularly as often arise immediately from the old wood are useless, and must be cleared away, wherever they are produced; except in such places where young wood is absolutely needful;—and even strong shoots that are destitute of fruit, and arise in places where they are not evidently wanted, should also be taken off.

When this is done, let all the bearing shoots, and all others that are necessary, be left in their proper places, in regular order—and do not stop any of the shoots now, but let each be left at full length for the present, so that all the branches, and fruit, may equally enjoy the advantages of sun and air.

After this dressing, observe, that all shoots that put out in any part of the vines, must be constantly rubbed off as soon as they appear, and no small shoots must be suffered to remain, unless it be to fill a vacancy.

STOPPING THE YOUNG SHOOTS OF VINES TO PROMOTE THE GROWTH OF FRUIT

About the beginning, middle, or any time in this month, when your vines are in full bloom, examine them carefully; and tie in all the shoots that you would have to bear fruit the next year;—you will likewise find a great number of fruit bearing shoots, which cannot be tied to the frame; let these also be minutely examined; and you will see some of them with one or two, and others with three branches of young grapes on them; let the tops of these shoots be taken off near the fruit; and where any small ones appear on the branches let these be entirely taken away. —Stopping the shoots in this manner will not only forward, but also greatly promote the growth of the fruit.

 FIG TREES

In the beginning, or at any time in this month, when you perceive suckers coming out from the bottom of your fig trees, let them be taken away as soon as they appear, least they rob both the shoots and fruit of their due nourishment.

Also if any young shoots appear on the old wood let them be cut away; but be careful not to cut the old wood, which will occasion the tree to bleed.

 ## WATERING NEW PLANTED TREES

New planted trees should be watered in dry weather; which frequently happens about the latter end of this month. This necessary work should be performed at least once a week; and give each tree about half a large watering pot of water.

JUNE

Work to be done in the Kitchen Garden

 SNAP BEANS

YOU MAY still continue to plant bush or snap beans, to succeed those planted in the former months.

The best sorts to plant at this season are the early white, black and yellow dwarfs;—they may be planted in rows, about twenty inches from each other, dropping the beans in the drills four inches apart.

It would be very proper, in dry weather, to steep the beans in soft water about six or eight hours before they are planted.—They will spring and take root much sooner and stronger.

You may also plant in this month the white runners; they will stand the heat better than the dwarfs, and bear more plentifully.—You must give them proper sticks for them to run up.

Let the bush beans that were planted last month, be frequently hoed; and let some earth be drawn up to the stems of those that require it.

 CABBAGES AND SAVOYS

Your cabbage plants, that were sown about the middle of April, will be fit to plant out early in this month, to the places where they are to cabbage.

For these plants prepare a piece of good ground, in the most open situation of your garden:—Dung it well with good rotten dung, if you can procure it; and dig it in evenly, laying the surface smooth; then mark out the ground for the plants, in rows about two feet or two feet and a half; and if your plants be of a very large kind, you may even allow them three feet from row to row, and two feet and a half from each other in the rows:—Observe that the distance for planting cabbage plants depends entirely on the goodness of the land.—The surface of the ground being laid even, and your rows all marked out, draw the earth up into small ridges or beds about six or seven inches high; and let the top of them be flat, observing at the same time to let these small beds or ridges range with the descent of the ground, if there be any; for if the water is suffered to lie in the alleys next month, when the heavy rains set in, the roots of the plants will be scalded; this is a very material circumstance which you ought to guard against.

It is very necessary also to observe, that the plants, at this season, should be planted out as soon after a shower of rain as possible; and if the weather should prove dry, give them now and then a little water every evening, till they have taken good root;—and should the day after planting prove very hot, which often happens in this month, it would be of great advantage to the plants to stick a small bush on the south side of them; which would not only protect the plants from the violence of the sun, but greatly promote their taking root.

You may still continue to sow cabbages and savoys, for winter use.

The seed, at this season, should be sown on beds about four feet wide; and if the weather proves dry, water them well every evening, both before and after the plants are come up; and if the beds had a temporary shade made over them, so as to admit a free circulation of air under it, this would be of great service to the plants.

 CAULIFLOWERS AND BROCOLI

About the beginning of this month you may sow cauliflowers and brocoli; and if proper care is taken of them they may succeed very well—Let them be managed much in the same manner as mentioned before of cabbage plants.

The cauliflowers and brocoli plants, which were

sown the beginning of last month, will be fit to prick out early in this.

For this purpose, prepare a piece of ground in an open situation; and divide it into beds about three feet wide; and plant on each bed six rows of the small plants, that you draw out of the seed beds, about five inches from each other in the rows.—Let them be watered in dry weather every evening, till they have taken good root.

 CARROTS AND PARSNIPS

At any time in this month, you may sow carrots and parsnips, for winter use, if you did not sow a sufficiency in the two last months.

It would be very necessary, to take the advantage of showery weather, for sowing the seed at this season.

Prepare for this purpose, a piece of good ground, in an open situation; divide it into beds about four feet wide, and sow four rows of carrots or parsnip seed on each bed.—[See April.]

Let the carrots and parsnips that were sown the last month, and in April, be frequently hoed, and properly thinned.

This is a work of more consequence than many imagine; for if the plants are once suffered to remain long crowded together, they will soon stunt each other, therefore let the business be not delayed.

If you design these carrots and parsnips to remain in the ground till November or December, the carrots should be thinned out at least to eight or nine inches from each other; and the parsnips to ten or twelve:—By strictly observing the above method you need not doubt of raising good roots of each kind. —[See April.]

LETTUCES

You may still continue to sow cabbage, Silesia, and brown Dutch lettuce, where a constant succession is required.

Prepare a piece of good soil, to sow the seeds at this season, in the lowest part of your garden; and take particular care to throw it up into high beds before you sow the seed; and observe that they are not sown too thick, for it is intended that the plants should remain in the seed beds till they are fit for use; for they will not bear transplanting at this season.

Let the lettuce plants be hoed and thinned that were sown last month, for they will now require it.

This work should be performed with a very even hand, cutting up all the small plants and weeds, and leaving those that are most promising, about seven or eight inches from each other, in regular order on the beds.

RADISHES

Sow a succession of radishes—the short top is the best sort to sow at this season; having prepared your ground, divide it into beds about four feet wide; and sow the seed thereon broad cast, but not too thick; and if the weather proves dry give them a little water both before and after the plants come up.

SMALL SALLADING

Sow mustard and cresses, at least every ten days or a fortnight, in the most shady part of your garden.

Sow these seeds in small drills or trenches, about four inches from each other; and if the weather should be dry, give the seed a little water every morning till it comes up, and the plants after they are up.

CELERY

Prick out celery plants if wanted, and not done in the last month; by pricking out these plants, they will grow strong and stockey, and will be much better to plant out next month for blanching, than those you would otherwise take out of the said bed.—[For the work see May.]

PULL ONIONS

Examine, towards the middle of this month, the forwardest crop of onions; when the leaves begin to wither, it is then the proper time to take the roots out of the ground. They must be managed in the following manner, which will serve also as directions for the same work next month.

These roots must be taken up in dry weather; and as you take them up, pull off their leaves; only observe to leave about four or five inches of the stalk to each root.—They should be spread to harden, upon a clean dry spot of ground, or upon a scaffold made for that purpose; let them lie ten or twelve days, remembering to turn them frequently that they may dry and harden regularly.

When they have lain a proper time, they may be gathered up, in a dry day.

Let them be very well cleaned from earth, and all outer loose skins; then bring them into the house, in dry weather, spread them evenly on the floor, and let them frequently be turned over the first two or three weeks.

Let the windows of the room be kept constantly open in dry weather;—observe, when you turn the onions over now and then, to pick out any that are decayed.

 PULL GARLICK AND SHALOTS

Pull up garlick and shalots, when full grown; this is known by the leaves—for when the roots are swelled as much as they will, the leaves begin to wither; let them be managed in the same manner as onions after they are taken up.

 CUCUMBERS, MELONS, SQUASHES, &c.

You may still continue to sow more cucumbers, melons, squashes, &c. for they will yet succeed very well.

They should now be sown in an open situation, on

hills of good earth, about twelve feet from each other.

Let the cucumbers, melons and squashes, that were sown last month, be now properly thinned; and leave not more than three or four plants on each hill.

 OKRA

Early in this month let your okra be properly thinned out; that is, let your plants be left at least three feet from each other in the rows, where the soil is rich,—Let them be frequently hoed; and let the ground be kept constantly loose about the plants, which will greatly promote their growth.

 TOMATOES

Your tomatoes will now begin to run; they, being of a procumbent growth, should have sticks to support them; which should not be very high, but strong and bushy; first let one stick be set in the middle of the hill, then put three or four more round the outside of the plants, to keep them from falling to the ground.

Fruit Garden

PEACH, NECTARINE AND APRICOT TREES

Where the peach, nectarine and apricot trees were not looked over, and put in proper order last month,

due attention should be now paid to them.—This
work should be attended to early in this month, and
followed with the utmost diligence till the whole is
completed; for where these trees are suffered to remain long in a wild and confused state, which they
will naturally fall into at this season, it would not
only prove detrimental, in a great degree, to the
trees, but would also very much retard the growth
and ripening of these kinds of fruit.—Therefore let
these trees be now in general looked over, taking care
to clear away all over grown and ill-placed shoots;
particularly such strong ones as arise from the
old wood, which you will often find in the middle of
the trees; the timely displacing such will not only
strengthen, but make more room for the useful
shoots; and also admit of a free circulation of air to
the fruit.

Let these shoots be taken away quite close to the
place from whence they are produced, except such as
grow out close to the fruit; which may be cut off
within half an inch of the branch.—Observe to leave,
in every part of these trees, a sufficient quantity of
the best shoots, for the purpose of bearing fruit the
next year;—leave also a plenty of the more regular
and moderate shoots that are well situated; observing
at the same time to keep the middle of the tree as open
as possible, to admit air among the branches.—Do
not shorten any of the shoots you intend to leave, for
the reason mentioned last month; but let them stand
at full length, both the large and smaller ones; and
take particular care to leave them in such a manner,

that the leaves may afford a moderate shade to the fruit in intense sunny days:—for it will thrive much better under a slight coverture of leaves, than when openly exposed to the sun; and the fruit will be better flavoured.

THINNING PEACHES, NECTARINES AND APRICOTS

The peaches, nectarines and apricots, still remaining too close upon the trees, should now be thinned; let the same rule be observed as that mentioned in the last month concerning these kinds of fruit.

SUMMER PRUNING ESPALIER TREES OF APPLES, PEARS, PLUMBS AND CHERRIES

The apple, pear, plumb and cherry trees will now have made strong shoots; which, if not gone over in May, it is now full time they should be examined and properly regulated.—Let these trees be looked over with good attention; and let them now be properly cleared of all useless and unnecessary shoots of the year; that is to say, all the luxuriant ones, wherever they appear, must be taken off close; all foreright shoots must be also cut away; and also such shoots as are produced in such parts of the trees where they cannot be properly trained in; and such as are not absolutely wanted to fill up the tree be displaced: but be careful to retain a moderate supply of the most regular and well placed shoots to train in, to chuse for winter pruning, by the rules here mentioned, viz.

In ordering these trees, it must be observed, that there is no need to leave a general supply of young wood, as in peaches, nectarines, &c. which bear their fruit always upon one year old shoots, and in consequence thereof, require a peculiar treatment.—But as the case is otherwise with the trees I am now speaking of, there is no necessity to leave, every summer, a general supply of young shoots in every part of the tree; for as to apples, pears, plumbs and cherries, their branches seldom begin to bear till they are two or three, and sometimes four or five years old; the branches of plumbs and cherries generally begin to bear at one and two years, likewise apples sometimes in the lower parts of these States: while the pears oftener bear from four to five year old spurs:—and when the branches of all these kinds have arrived to a fruitful state, the same bearers continue to produce fruit in more and greater abundance for many years: so that there is no necessity, after the trees are once furnished fully with bearing branches, to leave such a general and constant supply of young shoots above mentioned, as would be required on different trees which produce their fruit on shoots of the preceding summer's growth.—But notwithstanding it will be proper to leave here and there, in every tree, some of the best grown and well placed side shoots, together with the leader, to each branch, if there be sufficient room: this precaution should not on any account be omitted; for some of those summer shoots will most probably be wanted, to lay in, to supply some vacant place or other of the tree, in the winter pruning.

But where there appears to be an absolute want of wood in any part of these trees, do not fail, in that case, to leave, if possible, some good shoots in such vacant parts.

It is always the best method to leave the trees pretty full of proper shoots, at this season; they will be ready, in case they should be wanted, to fill up any vacancy, or to supply the place of old useless dead or worn out wood, when you come to prune in the winter; and such shoots as are not wanted may then be cut away.

Let all the shoots that are now left be trained at full length, and nailed or fastened up close to the frame, in a neat and regular manner all the summer.

 WATERING

Water should still be given, in dry weather, to new planted trees; and in particular to such as are planted late in the spring.

This work should be done at least twice a week in hot and dry weather; and give each tree one, two, three or four gallons of water in the evening in proportion to its size, and as its state may seem to require.

JULY

Work to be done in the Kitchen Garden

 BUSH OR SNAP BEANS

YOU MAY, at any time in this month, plant bush or snap beans to succeed those sown in the last.

The early sorts are preferable for this planting, such as white negro and yellow dwarfs.

Choose, at this season, a piece of ground in an open situation; and, if you can give it a moderate dressing, it will be the better; let the ground be well dug, and laid even; and if the weather is inclinable to be very wet, which often happens about this time, take precaution to guard against it, otherwise it may prove destructive to the crop.

Therefore while your land is fresh dug mark out the rows, about one foot eight inches from each other, and draw the earth with your hoe up into small beds or ridges, about four inches above the surface; then on these ridges or beds draw your drills, and plant your beans as directed in the former months.

But, on the other hand, should the weather prove dry, it will be necessary to steep them in soft water, for six or eight hours, before you plant them; they will in that case come up much sooner and stronger —it will be also requisite, when the ground is very dry, to water the drills, before you plant the beans.

But let it be observed that steeping the beans is necessary only in dry weather, and the drawing up the small beds or ridges, in a wet season.

Let the bush beans that were planted the last month be frequently hoed, and the ground be kept constantly loose between them, which will greatly promote their growth; and draw earth up to the stems of those that are advanced to the height of four or five inches, which will support and strengthen them.

 CABBAGES

The plants from cabbage seed, which was sown about the latter end of May, will be now fit to put out for good.

Make choice of a piece of rich ground in an open situation, and lay some good rotten dung thereon if it can be procured; dig it in, and lay the surface even; then mark out the rows, about two feet or two feet and a half from each other; and with a hoe draw the earth up into small flat beds or ridges, about six inches above the surface of the ground, and six inches broad on the top; and set the plants about two feet from each other—It is to be supposed that the water tables of the garden are lower than the trenches between the rows, by which means the water may be the more easily carried off, which would otherwise greatly injure the plants, if not wholly destroy them.

You may still continue to sow the seeds of cabbages and savoys where required; if the rain does not cripple them they will be fit to put out in six weeks after sowing, and will be particularly serviceable in town gardens.

For this purpose prepare a piece of ground, in a shady situation, but let it not be under trees; throw it up into high beds, and allow them good bold alleys; that water may not lie between the beds let them range with the descent of the ground.

 CAULIFLOWERS AND BROCOLI

About the beginning of this month, if not done in the last, transplant your first crop of cauliflowers and brocoli, where they are to remain till they are fit for use.

For this crop you should choose one of the best pieces of land your garden affords; and to have fine cauliflowers and brocoli you must give it a dressing with good rotten dung—and let it be spread even over the surface; dig it in, and lay the ground smooth; then mark out the rows about two feet and a half for the cauliflowers, and three feet for the brocoli; plant the former at two feet in the rows, and the latter two feet and a half: the ground being dug in a proper manner, draw the earth up into small beds or ridges, as before directed under the head of cabbages; and, if the weather should prove dry after planting, give them a moderate watering every evening, till they have taken good root; and if you were to stick a small bush on the south side of each plant the next morning after they are put out, (the evening being now the best time for planting) it would be of great service to them, by screening them from the intense heat of the sun.

You may still sow more cauliflower and brocoli seed, if you have not got a sufficiency of plants from your former sowing; they may be sown on a bed, as directed in last month; and should now have a temporary shade erected over them, which will not only break the violent heat of the sun, but also the heavy showers of rain which commonly fall, and cripple the young plants at this season.

If the weather should prove dry, after the sowing of the above seed, give them a moderate watering every evening till they come up, and every two or three days after they are up; for the plants at this time ought to be forwarded as much as possible in their growth, as the season for sowing them is almost spent.

 LEEKS

The leeks that were sown the beginning of last month will be fit, by the latter end of this, to plant in the places where they are to remain, till wanted for the use of the kitchen.

For this purpose dig a piece of ground in an open situation, and if you can give it a little dung it would be the better; divide it into beds about four feet wide; then draw some of the largest of the plants out of the seed bed; cut off the ends of the roots and likewise the leaves; and plant them, on the beds prepared to receive them, about six or seven inches distant from each other; and give them a moderate watering every evening till they have taken good root.

 ONIONS

Your spring sown onions will be fit to take up by the beginning of this month;—let the utmost attention be paid to this crop; for these are the roots you are to depend on for winter use; let them be housed as soon as they are quite dry and in order, and managed as directed in the former month.

 CARROTS AND PARSNIPS

You may still sow carrots and parsnips, if they are required;—they will yet succeed pretty well if you can prevent the sun from scalding their roots after they are come up, and the heavy rains from crippling them.

Clear the weeds, &c. from the ground where you intend to sow the seed; and give it some dung, if you can procure any—dig the ground a full spade deep—thus done, divide it into beds about four feet broad, and leave good bold alleys full fifteen inches wide and six inches deep;—sow four rows of carrot or parsnip seed on each bed: if the earth be dry when you sow the seeds, give the drill a moderate watering before you cover up, and then rake the ground smooth, and take the stones, &c. out of the alley.

Let those carrots and parsnips which were sown in the former month be constantly hoed, and the earth kept loose between the plants until the tops of them cover the ground; and also let those be thinned that require it.—[See April and May.]

ENDIVE

Towards the latter end of this month, you may sow endive seed, for the first crop.

Dig for this purpose a piece of good ground, in an open place; and divide it into beds about four feet wide, and sow the seed thereon, but not too thick, and rake it with an even hand;—should the weather prove dry, give the seed a little water till it comes up; and the plants now and then after they are up.

TURNIPS

About the middle or towards the latter end of this month, if the weather suits, sow your first crop of turnips.

For sowing this seed, choose an open situation— dig the ground, and sow the seed while it is fresh dug —let great care be taken not to sow the seeds too thick, but as regular as possible;—divide the ground into beds from four to ten feet wide, and allow good bold alleys; and let the beds range with the declivity of the ground, so as not to suffer any water to lie on the beds, or even in the alleys.

 LETTUCES

Dig a spot of ground, in an open situation, to sow more lettuce seed—the Silesia, and curled coss are the best sorts to sow at this season; and should be sown at least twice in this month, to have a constant and regular supply.

It is very difficult to raise lettuce to any degree of perfection in town gardens; they being in general too close and confined: and the heavy rains, that generally fall in this and the next month, often cripple the plants before they get strength.

Observe to sow the seed on high beds, about three or four feet in width; and let the alleys be broad and shelving, so that no water may lie in them.

 CELERY

You may, about the middle of this month, prepare some trenches, to plant out your first crop of celery.

For this purpose choose a spot of rich ground, and clear it well from weeds; then mark out the trenches about a foot broad, and allow three or four feet between the trenches; dig each out at this season about six inches deep, without shoveling the crumbs out at the bottom; place the earth that comes out neatly in the spaces between the trenches; observe to lay it equally, and spread it as even as possible;—then put in the bottom of each trench some good rotten dung, and dig it in.

Then take up some of the best plants from the seed bed, if you have not pricked any out—choose the strongest you can find, and trim the end of their roots, and the tops of the straggling leaves—plant them in a row along the middle of the trench, setting the plants about five or six inches from each other, and give them a good watering:—let this be repeated every evening in dry weather till the plants have taken good root.

 RADISHES

You may still continue to sow salmon, short top and turnip radishes, where a constant supply is required: but there is not much prospect of a great crop from this sowing, owing to the uncertainty of the weather. —If it sets in dry, the plants will be burnt up, if not constantly watered; and, on the other hand, the heavy rains that often fall now are very destructive to the young plants, together with the intense heat of the sun, which seldom fails destroying the greatest part of them before they arrive to perfection, unless they have a temporary shade made over them; which will break the violence of the rain, and also check the scorching heat of the sun.

For sowing radishes at this season prepare a piece

of ground in an open situation, and divide it into beds about three feet wide; and sow the seeds evenly: let it be observed that the alleys between the beds ought to be both deeper and wider in this and the following month than at any other time, in order to draw off all the superfluous water that may fall at this season.

SMALL SALLADING

You may now, sow where required, the different sorts of small sallading; such as mustard, cresses, rape, &c.

Where these small herbs are daily wanted, there should, in order to have a constant supply of such as are young and good, be some seeds sown at least once a week.

Prepare a small piece of ground in a shady situation, but not under trees; and sow the seeds in drills as advised in the former months; and if the weather should prove dry, let the seed be watered every evening till it comes up, and the plants also, till they are fit for use.

SPINAGE

Towards the latter end of this month, sow some spinage seed; it will be fit for use in the autumn.

The best sort to sow at this season, is the round seeded or the broad leaved kind.

Prepare a piece of good ground in an open situation; let it be well dug, and the surface laid even; and let it be divided into beds about four feet wide; and on each bed draw four drills—scatter the seeds thin in each—cover it lightly over with your hoe, and rake the surface even.

You may likewise sow a few radish seeds with the spinage; the former will come out before the latter wants hoeing.

Should the weather prove dry, it will be requisite to give the seed a moderate watering till it comes up; and the plants now and then after they are up.

 WATERING

Watering should, at this time, be duly practiced in dry weather, to all such plants as have been lately planted out, till they have taken root.

This work should be done always in the evening about two hours before sun-set that the water may have time enough to soak in before the sun comes on the plants the next day.

Fruit Garden

 PRUNE PEACH, NECTARINE, AND APRICOT TREES

In gardens where these trees have not yet had their summer pruning, that very needful work should be done early in this month; otherwise the fruit upon such trees will not only be small and ill formed, but also very bad tasted, in comparison to the true flavour of this fruit.

And besides retarding the growth, and debasing the taste of the fruit, it is also detrimental in a very great degree, to both standard and espalier trees, to neglect summer pruning until this time; and in particular peach, nectarine, and apricots, and such like trees as produce their fruit principally upon one year old shoots.

Besides, it causes great perplexity to the operator, to break through and regulate such a confusion of young shoots;—it also requires treble pains and labour, and cannot be executed with half the accuracy as when the work is commenced early in the summer.

There is a very great advantage in beginning early in the summer to prune, train and leave the useful shoots in their proper places; and at the same time to clear the trees from all that are ill-placed and luxuriant:—For when the useless ones are timely cut away, and the useful left in a regular manner all the summer, the sun, air and gentle showers will have a proper access, not only to promote the growth and improve the flavour of the fruit, but also to harden and ripen the shoots perfectly, which is absolutely necessary to their producing good fruit the next year.

But however, where there are standard and espalier trees still remain unpruned, do not fail to let it be done the beginning of this month.

Do not shorten any of the shoots at this time; but let every one be left at full length.

Look also again over such espalier trees as were pruned, and tied down the two last months; and see if all the proper shoots which were laid in before, keep firm to their places;—and where any of them have been displaced, or got loose, let them be tied, and nailed again close in proper order.

Likewise observe, if there has been any straggling shoots produced since last month, in places where not wanted, let them be also displaced.

It would also be very necessary to look over again, those trees that were pruned in April and May;—you will find on them a great number of useless shoots that are put out since that time, which should be cut away; in particular side shoots that have put out this summer's branches—let these be cut away also.

AUGUST

Work to be done in the Kitchen Garden

 PEASE

ABOUT THE BEGINNING, or middle of this month, you may sow pease for an autumn crop.

The best sorts to sow at this season, are the Charleton, or golden hottspur;—they being early kinds, will come forward before the winter sets in.

Let a piece of ground be prepared in an open situation; and if the weather is inclined to be wet, draw the earth up into flat ridges, or small beds, about four feet from each other: but if the ground be dry it will be proper to steep the pease in soft water, about eight or ten hours before you sow them.

 BUSH OR SNAP BEANS

About the beginning of this month, plant bush or snap beans for a general fall crop;—they will come in at a very good time for pickling:—Prepare a piece of good ground in a free and open situation; and if you can refresh it with a little manure, it would be the better;—let it be well dug, and the surface laid even: —As this season in general proves wet, it will be necessary to plant the beans on small flat beds, or ridges drawn up with a hoe, about a foot broad on the top, and five or six inches above the common surface, and draw some drills thereon about two inches deep, and plant the beans, and cover them over as directed in the last month.

You may plant any of the dwarf kind at this season, both the early and late;—tho' planted at the same time, you will have a regular succession; as the former will come in ten or twelve days sooner than the latter.

Let the beans which were planted in the last month, be frequently hoed, as plants of all kinds require it more now than at any other time, on account of the heavy rains that generally fall at this season, which wash and harden the ground much; and while it remains in this state the plants will not thrive until the earth is loosened.

Draw earth up to the stems of those beans that are advanced to the height of three or four inches, as they will stand in great need of it.

AUGUST

 CABBAGES

About the beginning, middle, or even at any time in this month, you may sow early York, sugar-loaf, and savoy cabbage seed.

The early cabbages sown at this season, will make handsome heads about the latter end of November, if managed as directed in the foregoing month.

The above mentioned sorts are well calculated for town gardens: for you may plant three of these to one of the larger kind of cabbages: neither will they be half so long on the ground.

Prepare a piece of rich ground in an open situation. —Having dug it well and laid your surface even, divide it into beds about three feet, or three feet and a half wide; remembering always at this season, to leave wide bold alleys, at least six inches below the surface of the beds, to keep the ground in wet weather as dry as possible;—sow the seed, but not too thick —cast a little earth over it, and rake the surface even: —if there was a temporary shade made of bushes, erected about four feet above the ground, and open on all sides to admit of a free circulation of air, it would be not only of benefit to the seed before it comes up, but also to the plants after they are up. —How often is the seeds-man abused, in this and the latter month, for disposing of bad seed, when in reality bad management is too often the cause. There are a number of indiscreet people that would sow seeds at this season when the ground is dry, without any shade; when three successive hot days would totally destroy the germination of all the seeds that are even buried at a proper depth.—How cautious then people ought to be of sowing any kind of seeds in hot weather without shading or watering them.

If you have any good cabbage plants of the large kind, that are now fit to put out, let a piece of ground be prepared to receive them.—After the ground is manured, well dug, and the surface laid even, mark it out in rows about two feet; or, if you have a plenty of garden room, two feet and a half from each other;—then with a hoe draw the earth up into small beds or ridges, about six inches high, and near a foot broad on the top; and set the plants about two feet from each other in the rows:—if the weather be dry, give them some water, and let it be repeated every evening till they have taken good root.

You may also transplant savoys at any time in this month, if you have plants and ground to spare—let it be manured, dug and managed in the same manner as before observed under the head of cabbages—only plant the savoy two feet from row to row, and twenty inches from each other in the rows; and give them a good watering after planting, if the weather continues dry:—let it be repeated every evening till they have taken root.

The plants that are put out at this time, will be handsomely headed in November and December; and will continue in excellent order to supply the table till January.

AUGUST

 CAULIFLOWERS AND BROCOLI

Prepare some good ground in the beginning of this month, if not done in the last, to plant out some brocoli and cauliflowers; an open spot not shaded by trees, should be preferred;—and spread some well rotten dung over the piece, and dig it in—this will be of great advantage to the plants.

Let them be planted in rows two feet and a half, or three feet asunder, and near the same distance in the rows; observe to draw the ground up in ridges or small beds, as described in the last month; and give each plant a little water should the weather be dry—this necessary work will forward their growth before the winter sets in, and will produce fine large heads in the spring.

Let the cauliflowers and brocoli that were put out in the last month, be now frequently hoed, and draw the earth up to their stems; as it will strengthen the plants, and greatly promote their growth.

 ONIONS

Towards the latter end of this month, sow onions for the first crop.

They may be sown in a bed very thick, in order to be transplanted out in October or November, where they are to remain till they are full grown.

CARROTS

You may also sow carrots at any time in this month, if you have a piece of ground vacant, and the weather suits.—[For the method see the two last months.]

SPINAGE

Prepare now some good ground (if neglected in the last month) for a general crop of spinage, to come in for use in November; this may be done any time in this month; but towards the middle, or near the latter end, is the best season for a certain crop: but delay it not till the month is out; for where a constant supply of spinage is required, it is necessary to sow two or three times between this and October.

Choose a piece of rich ground in an open situation; and after the ground is dug, and divided into beds about four feet wide, draw four drills on each bed, and sow the seed thereon; but let care be taken that it be not sown too thick—cover it over with your hoe, and rake the surface smooth—you may sow a small sprinkling of radish seed with the spinage.

Observe, it is the round seeded sort that is to be sown now; for this bears large thick and broad leaves, but it is not so hardy as the prickly sort.

TRANSPLANT CELERY

Transplant more celery: let an open spot be chosen: mark out the trenches, and prepare in the same manner as directed in last month. Get the plants: cut off the tops of their leaves, and trim the ends of their roots: plant one row in each trench about five or six inches from each other. Immediately after they are planted, let them be watered; and if the weather should continue dry, the watering must be duly repeated every evening untill the plants have taken root.

 ENDIVE

The endive that was sown last month, will be now fit to transplant.—Choose for this purpose a small piece of ground in an open situation; and if you can give it a little manure it would be much the better—let it be well dug, and the surface laid even; and divide it into beds about five feet wide, and plant four rows of the largest plants on each bed.—It will be also necessary (if the weather should prove dry) to give the plants a moderate watering every evening. —If you have not planted any cabbage or lettuce plants between your celery, it would be a very proper place for endive.

Let the ground be fresh dug between the rows, about two spades wide, and rake it smooth; then plant one row of the best plants you can find, on the seed bed, about ten inches or a foot from each other.

 TURNIPS

Early in this month sow turnips of any kind for autumn or winter use—but if you have not sown any before, the early Dutch is the best for the first crop; as they will come in a fortnight or three weeks sooner than the large sorts, and are also much sweeter and better for the table.

 HOEING TURNIPS

Your turnips which were sown last month, now want hoeing—this necessary work must not be delayed after the leaves of the young plants are arrived to the size of a copper:—The business of hoeing turnips is of more consequence than many are aware of; and must be performed in a very nice manner.—Prepare yourself with hoes made for that purpose, viz. For the small early sorts, six inches will be wide enough; and eight or nine inches for the large kinds.—Let the edge of your tools be sharp, so as to cut out all the plants that stand within the width of your hoe; and to leave the strongest plants six or seven inches from each other, and the larger kinds from nine inches to a foot.—By thinning the plants in this manner, it will greatly promote their growth, and also destroy the young weeds which are now coming up plentifully amongst them:—This work should be repeated at least every fortnight (until the leaves cover the ground) in order to keep the earth constantly loose between them: for you will find, that after every heavy shower of rain, the earth will be bound on the surface, and the plants will not thrive well till it is broken.

AUGUST

 POTATOES

Some time about the beginning of this month, plant potatoes for winter use.

For this purpose choose a piece of good ground in an airy situation, and give it some manure if you have any to spare—let the land be well digged, and the surface laid even—then mark out the rows about two feet and a half from each other, and draw the earth up into small beds about eight or ten inches broad on the top:—In the middle of these beds plant one row of the sets about ten inches or a foot one from the other: they may be either planted with a dibble about two inches deep, or you may draw drills with a hoe, and place the sets in them: let the part of the root which is cut be put downwards.

 LETTUCES

You may still continue to sow lettuces, to succeed those which were sown in the former month.—The seed at this time should be sown in a small piece of low ground, pretty thick, and watered every evening till it comes up; as it is intended for transplanting as soon as fit for that purpose.

 RADISHES

You may now sow more radishes; for where these roots are constantly required, they should be sown every fortnight at least, to have such as are young and good.

The salmon, short-top, and turnip radishes, are all proper sorts to sow at this season; and should be sown in beds about three or four feet wide, but not too thick: should the weather be dry let them be watered till they come up, and three or four times a week after they are up.

 SMALL SALLADING

You may still sow small sallading where it is wanted; such as mustard, cress, rape, &c.

Sow the seed in small drills, as directed in the former months; and let the ground be watered frequently till the plants come up, and in dry weather; and every other evening at least after they are up.

SEPTEMBER

Work to be done in the Kitchen Garden

 PEASE

L ET EARTH be drawn up to the stems of the pease that were sown last month, if not done before: for they will now require it; and it will strengthen them greatly.

Set sticks to them when they are arrived to the heighth of four or five inches; and let your sticks be from four to five feet high, which will be quite sufficient at this season.

If you have neglected sowing pease in the former month, you may venture to sow some early in this:— but this work should not be delayed: for the sooner they are planted the better.—[For the method see last month.]

 BUSH BEANS

Let the bush beans which were planted in August, be frequently hoed; and let earth be drawn up to their stems, for they stand in need of it.

If you have neglected planting bush or snap beans in the last month, it is not yet too late: the work should not be delayed, but done immediately.—[For the method see August.]

 CABBAGES AND SAVOYS

Towards the latter end of this month, transplant the early York, sugar-loaf, and savoy cabbage plants, sown in the last month:—Prepare a piece of good ground in an open part of your garden—manure it well, and spread it even over the surface; then dig it in, and plant the early York, about one foot eight inches from row to row, and eighteen inches in the rows—the sugar-loaf and savoys will require a little more room: that is, about two feet from row to row, and one foot eight inches along the rows.

Should the weather prove very wet, it would be necessary to draw the earth up into small beds or ridges, to protect them from the water; which would otherwise rot their roots if planted in the level surface.

If you have omitted sowing early York, sugar loaf, and savoy cabbages, in August, let it be not delayed but done as soon as possible; for the seed even if sown early in this month will make pretty cabbages by Christmas, if managed in a proper manner.

Let this seed be sown in beds, on an east or west border, but not in a south aspect, nor yet too thick —in dry weather water the seed every evening till it comes up.

About the latter end of this month, or early in the next, you will not fail to sow early York, sugar-loaf, and drum-head cabbage seed, to come early in the spring.

The seed that is sown now should be imported from Europe; for if you save it from the cabbages that are the growth of these States, they will run to seed in the spring almost to a plant—while the others are forming fine heads.—This doctrine tho' but little known, may be relied on as a fact, as I speak from experience, which no art or argument can confute— and however strange it may appear to some of my readers, I hope they will not censure me before they have made a fair trial on what I have advanced— Similar circumstances are to be met with in carrots, parsnips and turnips, as before observed.

CAULIFLOWERS AND BROCOLI

You may still continue to put out the plants of cauli- flowers and brocoli, if you have any that are good, and ground to spare—they will do very well in the lower parts of these States from this planting—the work ought not to be delayed, but done as soon as possible.

Let the ground be prepared, and the plants put out (as advised in the last month.)

Let the cauliflowers and brocoli that were transplanted before, be hoed as soon as they have taken good root: for nothing promotes the growth of all plants of this kind as hoeing them frequently, whether there are any weeds come up amongst them or not.

Towards the latter end of this month, or early in the next, sow cauliflower seed—the plants from this sowing if they come on well, and the winter does not kill them, will be fit to put out about Christmas; and will come in fit for use the beginning of May.

 TURNIPS

If you have not sown any turnips before now, let this work be attended to as soon as possible; and if not delayed too long, you may yet have a tolerable good crop.

The best sorts to sow at this time are the early Dutch, or red top—they will come in at a proper season, and are exceeding good for the table. Sow this seed much in the same manner as advised in the last month; and let care be taken not to sow it too thick, but as even as possible.—Let the turnips that are now fit for hoeing be duly attended to; and those which were hoed last month be gone over two or three times in this, as it will add greatly to their growth.

Choose out one or two of your steadiest hands, to

hoe turnips the first time; and make choice of boys for the second and third hoeings; by which means they will be improving, and in a short time they will be capable of performing the work with accuracy and dispatch.

 POTATOES

The potatoes which were planted the last month, will now want hoeing; and, about the middle of this month let some earth be drawn up to the plants, which will be of great service to them:—this work should be repeated every ten or twelve days till the roots begin to swell, and the tops nearly cover the ground.

 ONIONS

The season is now advancing for the sowing of onions for a general crop—about the middle of the month is a very proper time to execute this work.

Choose a small piece of good ground in an open part of your garden—dig it, and divide the same into beds about three or four feet wide—sow the seed thereon pretty thick, and cast a little earth over it, raking the surface of the beds smooth.

 CARROTS

If you omitted sowing carrots in the former months, it would be necessary (where these young roots are constantly required) to sow seed early in this month: if the weather proves mild, they will be fit for use the latter end of December.

Let those which were sown in the two former months be often hoed;—let them also be thinned that stand in need of it, which will forward the plants greatly.

 SPINAGE

Spinage may be sown at any time in this month, with the utmost prospect of success: but if the work has been neglected, the sooner some seed is put into the ground, the better for a general winter crop.

You may sow the seeds now on the east or west borders of your garden, in drills about nine inches one from the other—scatter the seeds thin in each: cover them, and rake the ground smooth.—Let the spinage that was sown last month be hoed as soon as you can plainly discover the rows—it will greatly encourage the growth of the young plants.

 ENDIVE

If you have now sown any endive in the former month, let this business be no longer delayed; for the plants ought to acquire strength before the winter sets in.

Transplant such endive as is fit to put out: If you have not planted any cabbages or lettuces between your celery, it will be a very proper place to receive some endive; and let the plants which were put out last month, either in beds or between celery, be hoed, at least every week; and the earth always be kept loose between the plants.

 CELERY

The celery plants which were put out the latter end of July, will now want a little earth to be drawn towards them; but let the utmost care be taken not to suffer it to fall into the hearts of the plants, which would choke them,—You may put out more celery if you have not a sufficient quantity out already: for they will do very well if put out by the middle of this month; and will be fit for use about the latter end of November.

Prepare a piece of good ground in the lowest part of your garden—dig out the trenches six or seven inches deep, and about four or five feet from each other—lay some good rotten dung in the bottom of each trench, and dig it in even—then plant one row of the best plants you can procure from your seed bed; or, if you have pricked any out, you will find them to be the best plants—cut off the ends of the straggling roots and the long leaves, planting them in the trenches about five or six inches from each other.

 LETTUCES

Early in this month transplant those lettuce plants that were sown the beginning of last month.—For this purpose choose a piece of good ground in the most airy part of your garden, and let it be manured as well as possible (for these plants delight in a rich soil and low situation at this season.)—Let it be dug and the surface laid even—then divide it into beds four feet wide—let the alleys be full six inches deep, and at least fifteen inches in width—rake the beds even, drawing all the stones and rubish into the alleys; and let it be taken away before you proceed to put out the plants.

Draw out of your seed beds some of the strongest plants which are thereon; and plant four rows of them on each bed, about nine inches from each other.

Having planted your first row, set your line down for the second; and put in your plants (not opposite) but in the opening between each plant of the first row, so that every three plants may form a triangle —by this method they will compleatly cover the ground before they crowd each other.

The lettuce plants that were put out last month, should be now often hoed, which will greatly encourage their growth:—for when you observe the ground to be bound on the surface, hoeing is always necessary—for this frequently happens after very heavy showers of rain;—and the plants will not thrive untill the earth is loosened.—Let care be taken not to draw the earth into the hearts of the plants when you are hoeing them.

You may sow lettuce seed the beginning of this month for a general crop of sallad after Christmas and the spring.

SEPTEMBER

You may sow any sorts at this time; but the best are the white curled coss, or Silesia, brown Silesia, cabbage, brown Dutch, green and white coss—they should be sown in beds as directed in the former month.

Let your lettuce plants in dry weather be duly supplied with water every evening; but let care be taken not to suffer it to run or wash the surface of the ground, as it will materially injure the plants.

 RADISHES

About the beginning or near the middle of this month, sow salmon, short-top, and turnip radishes, for a general autumn crop, for they will succeed very well.—Prepare for this purpose a piece of good ground in the most airy part of your garden, and let it be well dug and divided into beds four feet wide: sow the seeds thereon, but not too thick: cast a little earth over it; and if the weather should continue dry it will be necessary to give the seed a little water till it comes up, and the plants now and then after they are up—let those radishes that were sown in the last month be also watered in dry weather every evening, which will prevent their growing hot and stickey.

 SMALL SALLADING

You may still continue to sow small sallad where required—such as mustard, cress, rape, radishes, &c.—These seeds may be sown in the east border of your garden, or, in a bed on any of the squares, in drills, as observed in the former month—and in dry weather let them be watered till it comes up, and the plants sometimes after they appear above ground:—Remember that the evening is the best time for watering plants of all kinds at this season.

Fruit Garden

 STRAWBERRIES

Near the middle, or towards the latter end of this month, if you have a piece of vacant ground, and would wish to plant out some strawberries, it may now be done with great propriety.—These plants may either be put out in one of the squares, or on each side of your principal walk in the garden, by way of borders; and they will make a pretty appearance let them be planted where they will. The ground should be well manured, dug and divided into beds four feet wide, and allow full fifteen inches for the alleys, and let them be five or six inches deep. Let the old strawberry beds be well examined, and take up as many young plants as you have occasion for, but do not disturb the old stools which are by no means fit to make a new plantation; for let it be observed that there were certain runners left in April for this purpose, which may now be taken up, and after trimming off the ends of the roots and loose leaves, let them be planted on the beds prepared to receive them; and if the weather be dry give them a good watering to settle the earth about the roots of the plants.

There is one great advantage arising from the early planting of strawberries, and that is, that they will have time to get strength before the winter sets in; and will be in condition to bear a good crop of fruit the next spring.

OCTOBER

Work to be done in the Kitchen Garden

BUSH BEANS

L ET THE BUSH or snap beans that were planted in the last month, be frequently hoed; and let some earth be drawn up to those that are advanced to the height of four or five inches.

CABBAGES

If you have neglected to put out your early York, sugar-loaf, and savoy cabbage plants, in the last month, let the work be no longer delayed, for they are advancing in their growth, and ought to be planted out for good.

Choose a piece of ground in an open situation, and

give it some good rotten dung if it can possibly be procured: for let it be observed, there is no crop that requires manure more than cabbages, and the different kinds of cole worts. As soon as the ground is dunged let it be immediately dug, and the surface laid even, and raked as smooth as possible—you need not draw the earth up in ridges as recommended in the former months (unless the weather proves very wet, which seldom happens at this time) but let the plants be put out on the level ground, and the savoys and sugar loafs in rows about two feet wide from each other from row to row, and one foot eight inches one from another in the row; and the early York one foot eight by eighteen inches: If the weather proves dry give them a moderate watering till they have taken good root.

Let the cabbage plants of all sorts, that were put out in the two former months, be frequently hoed; and let some earth be drawn up to those that stand in need of it; which will strengthen them, and greatly promote their growth. But if you leave neglected to sow early York, sugar loaf, and drum-head cabbages in the last month, let it be no longer delayed: for the time is now advancing when this seed should be put into the ground. It ought to be sown in beds, in the same manner as directed in September.

 CAULIFLOWERS AND BROCOLI

If you have any good cauliflower or brocoli plants, that were not planted out in the last month, they may be put out early in this:—I have known them produce very good heads in Charleston from this planting—but they will not answer ten miles in the country.—On the islands near the sea, and in the towns of Beaufort and Savannah, or to the southward, they may be transplanted with some prospect of success, if your ground is rich and in good order. —Let these plants be put out at this season, in rows two feet from each other; and the same distance one from the other in the row.

Let the cauliflowers and brocoli that were transplanted in the former months, be now frequently hoed; and let the earth be drawn up to their stems as they advance in growth.

 TURNIPS

Let the turnips which were sown in the former month, be frequently hoed, and properly thinned; as it will greatly forward the late sown crops, which stand in much need of it.

 ONIONS

Towards the latter end of this month, the onions that were sown for a first crop will be ready to transplant out, where they are to remain till they are fit for use. —Choose a piece of good ground in an open situation; and lay some good rotten dung thereon; dig it in even, and rake the surface as smooth as possible

—then divide the ground into beds about four feet wide—draw out of your seed beds some of the largest plants that you can find—trim off the ends of their roots, and the tops of their leaves; and let four rows of these plants be put out on each bed, eight or nine inches from each other; and give them a good watering if the ground is dry.

 PLANT GARLICK AND SHALOTS

Towards the latter end of this month, or early in the next, you may plant out garlick and shalots.

Choose for this purpose a piece of good ground in an open situation, and lay some rotten dung thereon if you can procure it; and let it be dug in even and the surface laid smooth; then divide it into beds about four feet wide, and on each bed plant four rows of the roots about nine inches from each other, and let the upper part of the root be an inch beneath the surface of the earth.

 CARROTS

The carrots which were sown in the former months, if the tops of the plants do not cover the surface of the ground, let them be hoed at least every fortnight or three weeks, to keep the earth loose between the rows;—and let those that stand too thick, be properly thinned in due time.

147

 SPINAGE

If you have omitted sowing spinage for winter and spring use, let it be delayed no longer, but done as early in this month as possible.—The sort I would recommend for this sowing, is the prickly seeded: and if the east border of your garden is vacant let it be prepared for this crop—sow your seed in drills eight or nine inches (cross-ways the border) from each other, but not too thick.

Let the spinage that was sown in the former months, be duly hoed and weeded; and let the early crops be thinned out so as to leave the plants standing single four or five inches from each other.—Where this work is executed in proper time, the plants will always produce broad and thick leaves.

 ENDIVE

Near the middle or towards the latter end of this month, take the advantage of a dry day to tie up some endive to whiten.

Make choice for this purpose of some plants of the most forward growth: gather the leaves up evenly in your hand, and let them be tied together a little above the middle, with a small band of moss or a soft string, so that it may not cut the outside leaves of the plants.

If you have plenty of endive plants, and have not put as many out as you could wish, let this business be attended to as early in this month as possible; and

148

let the plants be put out as directed in the former month; observe, if your plants are of a large size to cut off the ends of their roots, and the tops of their straggling leaves, before you plant them.

Let the endive plants that were put out in the last month, be frequently hoed, until they are forward in their growth.

 CELERY

Take advantage of a fine day, and earth such celery as require it.—Let the earth be well laid up to the plants, and within six or eight inches of the top of their leaves.—Let this work be performed with the utmost care; and lay your earth up gently to the plants least it falls into their hearts and choaks them. —This earthing up should be repeated at least three or four times in this month; as it will not only promote their growth, but their blanching also.

 LETTUCES

Near the middle, or towards the latter end of this month, let the south border of your garden be got ready to receive some lettuce plants, to come in for use early in the spring—supposing the border to be about four feet wide;—plant thereon four rows of the best plants that you can find on the seed bed, about nine or ten inches from each other; and if the weather should prove dry, let them be duly watered till they have taken good root.

Let the plants that were put out in the last month be often hoed, and the surface of the ground always kept loose between them.

 RADISHES

You may yet sow radishes where required, for winter use; and at this season in a sheltered situation; in beds about four feet wide, or on a border that is open to the sun: and in dry weather let the plants be watered in the evenings till they get strength.

 SMALL SALLADING

Where small sallading is required, you should now sow it on a border open to the sun, in drills, as directed in the former month.

 ARTICHOKES

Near the middle, or towards the latter end of this month, let your artichokes be well examined, and give them their winter dressing.

Take away all the earth round the stool, or plant about two feet wide and six inches deep, clean to the roots:—This being done, provide yourself with a hard piece of wood about six inches long, two inches wide, and half an inch thick;—make one end of it as sharp as possible; and let all the shoots or suckers on the old stool be well examined—then with the wooden instrument take away all the smaller shoots quite close to the stock from whence they arise, (which have sprung up since the last dressing)—except four or five of the largest that are to be left; and let the loose straggling leaves be cut off but not close to the stock; then lay on the roots, and crown off the stool between the remaining suckers or shoots, a wheelbarrow full of good rotten dung, and spread it even where the earth was taken out—then let the earth be put back again on the dung, raising it about the remaining plants full six inches higher than before the work was begun; and let the utmost care be taken that the loose earth do not fall into the hearts of the plants, which will greatly injure them.—To prevent this it would not be improper to tie the leaves together of those suckers that you do intend to leave till the work is executed.

Let it be observed, that the four or five suckers or shoots which are left, are not all to remain to bear heads the next year—for three is quite sufficient for the strongest stool; and the other two are left as a reserve, in case you should be in want of plants to make a new plantation in the spring.

By this fall dressing it will strengthen the plants greatly that remain; as I may justly suppose there are four times as many suckers taken away as are suffered to remain.

 ASPARAGUS

Towards the latter end of this month, let your asparagus beds have their winter's dressing.

In the first place let all the stalks be cut off quite close to the ground, and carried away: then let both the alleys and beds be hoed, and the ground raked as clean as possible; and the weeds and litter if any, be all taken off.

The beds and alleys being now clean, provide yourself with a fork for the purpose of dressing the asparagus beds—it should be about ten inches wide, and contain three tines, each about a foot in length, and an inch and a half broad; the back part perfectly flat, and the fore side convex, or a small rising in the middle of each tine—let the ends be blunt, so that they may not wound the crown of the roots.—Let the beds and alleys be forked up three or four inches deep, and the earth laid smooth and even—then with your rake draw an inch or an inch and a half of the earth off each bed into the alleys—lay some good rotten dung thereon about four inches thick, spreading it even—dig out the earth in the middle of the alleys a full spade deep, and fifteen inches wide, covering the dung with the same (you have before put on the beds) as even as possible, and rake the surface smooth.

By this management your asparagus beds will lie dry and warm all the winter, and produce fine large buds in the spring—You may plant on these beds some endive, or early York cabbages; but remember that whatever crop you plant on your asparagus beds must be taken off by the tenth of February, in order to give them their spring dressing.

Fruit Garden

 STRAWBERRIES

Early in this month is a good time for making new plantations of strawberries, as they will soon take root, and will acquire strength to bear fruit in the next spring.—The sooner this work is done the better.

You may either plant them in beds on the quarter of your garden, or in the borders of each side of the principal walk;—but let them be planted where they will (if you would wish to have good fruit) the ground must be well manured.—Dig your land a full spade deep, and divide it into beds four feet wide—then put out four rows of the best young plants you can find on the old beds.—If you remember there were some left in April for this purpose, which will be by this time fine plants; tho', to have them strong, and bear good fruit in the spring, it would be necessary to take them up with small balls of earth to their roots, and immediately planted on the beds prepared to receive them—and if the weather be dry give them a good watering to promote their growth, as well as to settle the earth about the roots.

RASPBERRIES

At any time in this month you may plant out raspberries where wanted.

Choose for these plants the lowest part of your garden; for they delight in low moist land; observe, never to suffer the water to lay on or between the beds, either in summer or winter.—If you would wish to have large, and good flavoured fruit, it would be proper to give your ground a good dressing with manure when you put out the plants.

The land being well manured, and dug a full spade deep, repair to the old beds, and take up some of the best young plants that can be spared.

It would be very imprudent to destroy the old beds the same year you make your new ones; as they will bear but little for the first and second season: tho' the third year they will come into full bearing, and produce fruit plentifully:—Therefore, as I observed above, take out only such young plants as can be best spared, and will not injure your crop, for the ensuing year.—You will find many young plants round the outside of the old beds, which (if not taken up to make new plantations) must be destroyed—let it be observed that the old plants which bore fruit the last year, are not proper to be planted out; for they will not produce fruit more than one season, when they die, and are succeeded by young shoots every summer:—It is these and these only, that I mean should be planted out to form new beds.

Having procured a sufficient number of young

plants, trim off the ends of the straggling roots, and one-third part of the young shoots, and plant them in rows four or five feet one from another; and about a foot or fifteen inches from each other.

Let the old raspberry beds be examined, and let all the old branches be taken out, and the young shoots properly arranged, and the weeds which are now on the beds be taken away, and the earth loosened between the young plants that are left—lay in some good rotten dung betwixt them, and let the alleys be now dug a full spade deep, and three feet wide, close up to the plants; and as you are digging between the rows, cast a little earth over the dung: by so doing the raspberry beds will look neat all the winter, and will be in a fair way of producing a good crop of fruit next season.

NOVEMBER

Work to be done in the Kitchen Garden

 PLANTING EARLY BEANS

NEAR THE MIDDLE, or the latter end of this month, you may plant some beans to come early the succeeding spring.

Those which are planted now, if they survive the winter's frost, &c. will be fit for use early in April.

The Mazagon bean is the best to plant at this season; for they will come up earlier then any other sort, and are excellent bearers tho' but of an humble growth; and they will stand the winter better than the larger kinds.

A warm border under a south wall, is the best situation to plant those beans at this season.

They should be planted in rows across the border

—that is, provided the border is five or six feet wide; observing that the rows are to be two feet asunder, which will be room enough for this sort.—The beans should be planted four or five inches from each other in the rows, and near an inch and a half deep.

You may also plant one row lengthways of the border, within two or three inches of the wall or fence: these will sometimes outlive the winter, when those at a greater distance from the wall, &c. are destroyed.

But, if the border is narrow, you had better plant two rows only lengthways; that is, one row near the wall, and the other about two feet and a half from it.

They may be planted either with a blunt dibble putting them in about an inch and a half, or near two inches deep; or you may draw drills that depth, and drop the beans therein; drawing the earth an equal depth over them, and rake the ground smooth.

In planting early beans, it often proves successful first to sow them pretty thick in a bed of rich earth; and when they come up a little height, transplant them into the borders.

The method is this:—Dig a bed about three or four feet broad, of good earth, in a warm corner of your garden.

The ground being dug, draw the earth off about an inch and an half or near two inches in depth equally from the surface, half to the one side and half to the other.—This done, scatter the beans thereon about an inch asunder, and immediately cover them over with the earth that was drawn off for that purpose:

or you may with your hoe draw broad flat drills cross-way the bed, and scatter the beans pretty thick, and cover them over with earth equally; and if severe frost should prevail in their infant state while remaining altogether in this, they can readily be protected with a few pine tops till they are fit to transplant.

When the beans are come up an inch and a half or two inches high, they should then in mild weather, be transplanted into the above mentioned borders, taking them carefully out of the seed-bed with their full spreading roots, and as much earth as will hang about them—pull the old beans at the bottom, and trim the end of the perpendicular root, and then plant them in rows in the same manner and at the same distance as before directed; observing to close the earth well about every plant—they will soon take root and grow freely.

One reason for this practice is, the best of gardeners allow, that the beans which are transplanted, will come in sooner by a week or ten days than those that are not, though the seed be put in the ground the same day.

 SOWING PEASE

About the middle of this month, sow pease for your first crop—if they escape the frost they will come for use early in April.

The early hotspurs are the proper sorts to sow at this time.—Choose seeds that are fresh and new.

There are several sorts of the hotspurs, such as the

golden, Carleton, Reading, &c. These I would recommend to sow for the first crop.

A warm south border, under a wall or fence, is the
most proper place to sow them in at this season—the
seed must be sown in drills, either lengthways or in
rows, athwart the border, according to its breadth:
where it is but narrow, draw one drill only lengthways at the distance of one or two feet from the wall
or fence, and scatter the pease therein pretty thick,
but as regular as possible—cover them up immediately with earth about an inch and a half deep, and
rake the ground even.

Where your border is five or six feet wide, it would
be proper to sow the pease in drills cross-ways the
same, about four feet distant from each other: and if
you intend they should run on sticks, you may plant
a row of cabbage or lettuce plants between them.

 CABBAGES

If you have neglected to put out any early or savoy
cabbage plants in the former month, and have good
plants and ground to spare, it may be done at any
time in this month, and will make fine heads early in
the spring without the least danger of running to
seed, as the large kinds are apt to do.—If the ground
be good where you have sown your first crop of early
pease, you may with propriety put out a row of these
plants between each row of pease, about sixteen or
eighteen inches from each other.

 ONIONS

If you have not put out any onions in the former month, it should be done as soon as possible in this.

Let a piece of ground be prepared to receive them: and after it is dug and divided into beds about four feet wide, cut off the ends of the roots as well as the tops of the long leaves, and plant four rows of them on each bed, about nine or ten inches one from the other in the rows.

Let the onions which were planted out in the last month, be frequently hoed, as it will be of infinite service to the young plants.

 LETTUCES

Lettuce plants which are designed to remain in the beds where sown for winter use, should now be cleared of weeds, and thinned where you find them too close.

Those plants which were sown in September, should now be transplanted into a warm south border, in order to come out for use early in the spring.

 RADISHES

Some time in this month sow some short-top radish seed, and if they survive the frost, they will be fit to draw early in February; and tho' there is but little hopes of their succeeding, yet where radishes are desired early, it will not be improper to sow a few to take their chance.

 SOWING PEASE

Let this seed be sown in a warm border near a walk or fence; observing to sow it pretty thick, and in a fair, dry day.

 SMALL SALADING

You may sow small salading in a sheltered situation: such as mustard, cresses, rape, &c. where required.

 CELERY

When the weather is open and dry, you should earth up your celery to blanch.—Break the earth well, and lay it up to the plants within six or eight inches of the tops of their leaves.

In performing this work let care be taken not to lay the earth too hastily to the plants, as it may be the means of forcing it into the hearts of them, which would occasion the plants to rot.

 ARTICHOKES

If your artichokes did not get their winter's dressing in October, it should be no longer postponed; for the sooner the work is performed the better.

The earth should be opened round the roots, and all the useless plants taken off; leaving four or five of the strongest suckers or shoots on each stock—lay some good rotten dung round them: when they should be earthed up and managed in the same manner as recommended in the month of October.

 ASPARAGUS

Where your asparagus beds were not forked and dressed up in the last month, let it be done early in this.

The stalks should be all cut away quite close to the ground; and the weeds which are on the beds or in the alleys, be hoed and raked to the ends of the same; and carried immediately out of the garden: then let them be forked up; the dung laid on; and the work executed as directed in the former month.

Fruit Garden

PRUNE LARGE-GROWN APPLE AND PEAR TREES

Towards the latter end of this month, let the apple and pear trees in the orchard, be well examined; and all dead, decayed, and worn out branches, be cut away; together with all the suckers and superfluous shoots which often arise out of the old limbs in the middle of the trees—and where you find the bearing wood too thick, and growing together, let it be taken out, in order to give room to such as you intend to remain to bear fruit, as well as to admit a free circulation of air among the branches.

The business of pruning old fruit trees is of more consequence than many are aware of; and require much judgment in performing the work:—Let the branches be regularly thinned, and as even as possible.

PRUNING PEACHES, NECTARINES, AND APRICOTS

This work may be done towards the latter end of this month; tho' you may execute it with equal success in the next.—[See January.]

STRAWBERRIES

If you have not transplanted any strawberries before now, and would wish to have them produce a crop of fruit the next season, the work should not be longer delayed, but put in practice as soon as possible.

Early in this month let the old beds or borders of strawberries be carefully looked over, and all the dead runners, leaves, &c. be cut off and taken away, as well as all the useless plants where too thick, be taken out, and the earth loosened about those which remain.—Let good rich earth or very rotten dung be conveyed between the plants, which will not only strengthen them, but enrich the land so as to look

163

neat all the winter, and produce fine fruit in the spring.

 RASPBERRIES

If your raspberries were not put out in the former month, the earlier done now the better; and let them be planted in rows as before directed.

Also let the old raspberry beds be well examined, and the dead branches which bore fruit the last year taken out; and the young shoots properly thinned—throw some good rotten dung between them, and dig the alleys as mentioned in October.

 PLANTING FRUIT TREES, &c.

Towards the latter end of this month you may plant out fruit trees; such as peaches, nectarines, apricots, apples, pears, plumbs, cherries, and grape vines—and let the same rules be observed as mentioned in January.

DECEMBER

Work to be done in the Kitchen Garden

 BEANS

ABOUT THE MIDDLE of this month prepare some good ground in a sheltered situation, for a successional crop of beans.

If you have not planted any before this period, let some of the mazagons be put in as early in this month as possible.

You may also plant some of the long podded, and Windsor, at the same time; as they will succeed each other in bearing.

Let the mazagons be planted in rows, two, or two and a half feet—the long podded two and a half, to three feet—and the Windsor three, or three and a half feet from row to row, and a proper distance in the rows, viz.—The first sort three inches—the second five inches—and the latter eight inches from each other.

If you have any beans that are up about two or three inches above the ground, let some earth be drawn up to their stems.—This work should be done in a mild, fine day, when the surface is perfectly dry: By this method you will not only preserve your plants in a great measure from the frost, but will support and strengthen them.

 PEASE

Sow more pease about the middle of this month, to succeed those which were sown in November; and in order to have a regular supply for the table.

If you neglected to sow any in the last month, do not delay it now; for the sooner you perform this business the better.—I would recommend the early kinds at this season, which will come forward with some prospect of success, and nearly as soon as those sown in the former month; as they are not so likely to be injured by the frost, and will probably bear a much greater crop.

Towards the latter end of this month, you may sow in a sheltered situation, some marrowfats and sugar pease.—These sorts will require sticking when they are three or four inches above the ground; and as they run very stately, your sticks ought to be at least five or six feet high; and your plants five or six feet from row to row; and not so thick in the rows as the early kinds.

This distance will appear very great at first; but be assured that your crop will be much the better for it, as it will admit of a free circulation of air between the rows.—You may if you think proper, plant cabbage plants between each row of pease.

Let the pease which was sown last month, have some earth drawn up to their stems, as it will strengthen them greatly, and prevent the wet weather from rotting them near the ground.—If you was to stick a row of pine or any other ever-green bushes betwixt the rows, it would be of infinite service in breaking the cold wind, which very often cuts off the early crops of pease.

 CABBAGES

Near the latter end of this month, the cabbage plants that were sown in October, will be by this time fit to plant out.

Choose a piece of good ground in a sheltered part of the garden; and lay on it some good rotten dung, and dig it in a full spade deep—lay the surface even, and rake the stones away if any; and put out the early York, cabbage plants in rows, about two feet from each other from row to row, and twenty inches in the rows; and let the sugar loaves be planted two feet every way; and allow the large kinds two feet and half by two feet.—If this crop is properly managed, they will make fine heads in April and May.

If you have a plenty of cabbage plants which were raised from English seed sown in September or October, it would be very adviseable to plant some between the rows of early beans and peas, to cut up for use in March, when you will find greens scarce—let it be observed that the ground ought to be always fresh digged before you put out these plants this matter is of more consequence than many people are aware of.

CAULIFLOWERS

Towards the latter end of this month, if your cauliflower plants (which were sown in October) are grown to a good size, let some of them be put out on the south border of your garden, if it is vacant—if not, the most warm and sheltered place that you can conveniently spare—let it be well manured, and dug a full spade deep—rake the ground even, and put out the plants in rows full two feet from each other.

The cauliflower plants which were put out in May and June last, will now begin to show their heads—you should therefore be very careful in protecting them from the frost.—For this purpose provide yourself with a number of hay, straw, or moss bands, well twisted together, binding the same round the stalks of your plants, beginning at the bottom close to the ground till you come up to about one third part of the leaves—let care be taken that you do not wind it too light round the leaves; but let the band be rather slack so as to afford the head sufficient room to swell;—you may tie the leaves together near their tops; for by this treatment you will not only preserve the cauliflowers from the frost, but will be the means also of rendering them perfectly white and beautiful to the eye.

Let the bands that are tied round the leaves be frequently examined; and see if the head has sufficient room to swell: if you find the band too tight, let it be loosened that the head may grow free and easy.

 BROCOLI

Let the ground between the last planted crop of brocoli be now hoed for the last time, and all the leaves which are fallen off between the rows taken away; and remember to let some earth be drawn up to the stems of those which require it.

 RADISHES

Towards the latter end of this month, sow some short-top radishes for an early crop.

Let a good piece of ground be prepared as open to the sun as possible; and if your south border is not engaged, it would be the most proper place to sow your seed in at this season.

The border being properly manured and dug, sow the seed broad cast pretty thick: you may also sow a sprinkling of carrots with your radishes; for if one should fail the other may come on—the latter will arrive to perfection and fit to be drawn before the carrots are got to any size: therefore, should they both succeed, the growth of the one will be no impediment to the other.—If it is not convenient for you to sow carrots, spinage may be sown with an equal prospect of advantage.

 LETTUCES

Let a small piece of good ground be prepared towards the latter end of this month, (as open to the sun and as sheltered from the cold winds as possible) in order to sow some lettuce seed.

The best sorts for this sowing, are the brown Silesia cabbage, and brown Dutch, they being the most hardy kinds.

Let the seed be sown pretty thick and even—cast a little earth over it and rake the surface smooth.

Should the weather prove frosty after the plants are up, it would be very necessary to cover them over while in an infant state, every night with pine, or other ever-green bushes, which will in a great measure protect them from the frost, as well as forwarding their growth.

The lettuces which are out in beds or borders, should be now kept perfectly clean of weeds, and the ground often loosened between them, which will encourage their progress.

Was you to cover even these with bushes as above, in frosty nights, it may be the means of saving them frequently from destruction.

DECEMBER

 SMALL SALADING

Where small salading is required, you should sow some at least every ten or twelve days, in a situation that is open to the sun; and in drills as directed in the former months—should there be any appearance of a frost, it would not be amiss to lay straw or bushes lightly over the plants every night, as it will greatly preserve and cherish them.

 SPINAGE

Let the beds and borders of spinage be kept perfectly clean of weeds, and the earth frequently loosened between the rows.

Where your plants are too thick, let them be properly thinned so as to stand not less than three or four inches from each other.

In gathering spinage let it be observed, that the large broad leaves should be cut first; and care ought to be taken that you do not injure the small ones, so as to destroy the whole at once.

 ONIONS

If you have not already planted out your onions, let it be no longer neglected; and the earlier the work is attended to in this month the better.—Let a piece of good ground be prepared for them, and the plants put out as advised in the two former months.

The earliest planted onions should be now kept

free from weeds, and the ground hoed frequently between them, which will greatly forward your plants.

 CARROTS

If the weather is mild and dry towards the latter end of this month, let a piece of ground be put in proper order to receive some carrot seed—the best sort for this sowing is the early horn or short orange; as they will come in for use near a month sooner than the long orange.

It would be very necessary to give your ground a moderate dressing with good rotten dung turned in well, which divide into beds four feet wide, sowing four rows of carrot seed on each bed, but not too thick —you may if you choose, sow a sprinkling of short top radishes with your carrots.

Let it be observed, that it must be the true orange carrot seed that is to be sown at this season: for if you sow the pale degenerated kind, it will be running to seed in May—when the roots from the European seed will be in their highest perfection.

 CELERY

Make choice of a fine dry day to earth up such celery as stand in need of it.—In performing this work great care should be taken that the earth do not fall into the hearts of the plants, by which it would greatly injure their growth, if not entirely destroy them.

DECEMBER

Should severe weather now set in, let your plants which are in the ground be carefully protected from the frost, by laying straw or some other covering that may be most convenient over the rows:—But if the ground should be very wet where your celery is planted, let some of the best of it be taken up and put into a dry, warm border, pretty thick, which you may take up for use whenever required.

 ENDIVE

Let the beds or borders where your endive was put out, be looked over, and tie up some of the largest plants.

Gather the leaves up regular in your hand, and tie them together a little above the middle, as close as possible, with a small moss band, or some strong bass matting; then with a small hoe draw up the earth close round the plants.

Should the weather prove severe and frosty, it would be very proper to take some of the plants from the beds that you have tied up; and let them be put into a south, dry border, in order that they may whiten.

In performing this work, take care that you do not cover the endive wholly over, but lay them into the earth within an inch of the tops of their leaves—and if the weather should be very wet, it would be proper to lay a plank over the plants to protect them from the heavy rains which would otherwise perhaps cause them to rot.

 ARTICHOKES

If the artichokes were not dressed up and properly managed in the last month, it should be no longer postponed; for it is now high time this work was done.—[See Oct.]

 ASPARAGUS

If your asparagus beds were not forked, dunged and dressed in the last month, it should be done as soon as possible in this.—[See October.]

If you recollect I recommended cabbage and lettuce plants to be put out on the asparagus beds in October last, after they were dressed; but it will now be too late in the season—for before your cabbages or lettuces (on these beds) would arrive to any perfection, they would require their spring dressing.

Fruit Garden

 PRUNE PEACH, NECTARINE AND APRICOT TREES

At any time in this month you may prune peach, nectarine and apricot trees; either dwarfs, espaliers or standards.

Let the trees be well examined, and all the useless shoots taken out, leaving the prime bearing ones at proper and regular distances; tho' if the trees be young and in a weakly state, let the shoots be shortened according to their strength: but if strong and vigorous, let them be managed as directed in January.

PRUNING OLD STANDARD APPLE AND PEAR TREES

If you have omitted pruning the old standard trees in the orchard, let this busness be now attended to; and displace all dead and decayed limbs that you may find in any of the trees; and let the young branches be properly thinned.

PRUNE PLUMB AND CHERRY TREES

You may also prune your plumb and cherry trees at any time in this month, if not done before.

Let it be observed that these trees do not bear their fruit from the last year's shoots (the morrell cherry excepted) but are produced generally from short spurs, sometimes two, three and four year's old; which should never be cut off but in some particular cases; but where these short spurs are forced by bad management, they will produce strong and vigorous shoots; the most irregular and unkind of which should be cut away; for the more you stop them, the more strong the shoots will become; and as long as you continue shortening the shoots at this season, be assured they will not produce any fruit-bearing spurs.

THE GARDENER'S CALENDAR

PRUNING YOUNG VINES THE FIRST YEAR AFTER PLANTING

The young vines which were planted out in the last season, should be now looked over; as they will probably have produced some (more or less) young shoots, the last summer.

These shoots should be all shortened within three eyes of the old wood, in order to make them put out with more vigour the next year.

PRUNING VINES THE SECOND YEAR AFTER PLANTING

As these vines were headed down very short the first year after planting, it is to be supposed that some of them have made three, four, and perhaps six fine and strong kindly shoots, eight or ten feet long.—These shoots, some over-wise people will lay in six or eight feet the second year—but such practice I by no means approve of: for the running them out so long before the plants are well established in the ground, will weaken them so much, that with all the art you are possessed of, it will be three or four years before your young vines will have acquired sufficient strength to produce good wood, without which there will be no prospect of fine fruit; therefore let the shoots be shortened the second year also, to within four or five eyes of the last year's wood; and the third season they will with proper care cover an arbor eight feet wide and ten feet high, with fine fruit-bearing shoots.—By this treatment your vines will acquire proper strength, and may probably produce some fine fruit the next summer.

PRUNING VINES THIRD YEAR AFTER PLANTING

By this time your vines will have acquired strength, if managed as before directed; and may have produced on each plant from eight to twelve fine bearing shoots, which should be also shortened according to their strength, leaving the strongest of them after pruned, at least five feet; and if very strong, six feet will not be too much.

Then let them be tied to the frame ten inches or a foot from each other:—Tho' this distance may seem great at this season, you will find your arbor compleatly shaded in the summer.—For the further management of these, I refer you to the next head on pruning old vines.

 PRUNING OLD VINES

If the vines were not pruned last month, let this necessary work be no longer delayed, but done as soon as possible; it being now a proper time for performing it.

In the first place let all the last summer's shoots which have sprung out of the old wood and branches be cut away; except in such particular places where they are absolutely wanted in the ensuing year: in such a case only they are to remain; but let them be shortened with two or three good eyes from the old wood.—By cutting the shoots so short it will be the means of their producing strong and kindly ones, which may probably prove fruitful the summer after next.

Observe in the next place, that all the short shoots which were suffered to remain in the last spring (for the purpose of bearing fruit only) should be now examined; and the most weakly and ill-placed of them be cut away; leaving the prosperous and most healthy shoots about ten or twelve inches from each other; and shortened so as not to have more than one or two good eyes (or as the gardener's call them spurs) to your vines; which will produce good fruit in the next season.

Thirdly and lastly, let all the shoots which were laid in the last summer, be carefully looked over; and all the side shoots from the principal bearing young branches be cut away quite close from whence they proceed; as they will neither bear good fruit, nor produce good wood, being always of a rambling and irregular growth.—This being done, shorten the shoots which are left, agreeable to the state and strength of each, as in the following manner.

Your young shoots will now require great attention, and must be shortened accordingly:—The most weakly should be cut back within three or four eyes of the old wood, in order to render them strong and healthy by the ensuing summer;—those of a middling strength should be taken off within five or six eyes, whilst those that are strong and luxuriant may be (where there is sufficient room) permitted to remain with eight or twelve, and even from twelve to sixteen eyes; tho' let it be observed, that this treatment is only intended for old grown grape vines.

 PLANTING OF VINES

At any time in this month you may plant out young vines where required.

Choose for this purpose some good young plants of one and not more than two years old.—If you put them out for an arbor (which is the most approved method) let holes be dug where you intend your plants to grow, about three feet wide and eighteen inches deep—put therein a barrow full of rich earth mixed with some good rotten dung, planting the young vines near the frame about five or six feet from each other, and pressing your foot gently round the plant to fix the earth.

Planting Fruit Trees

APPLES, PEARS, PEACHES, NECTARINES, APRICOTS, PLUMBS AND CHERRIES

At any time in this month you may transplant any of the above fruit trees by way of espaliers, in your garden.

If you plant plumbs or cherries, to train on a

frame, they should be put out about fourteen feet from each other, and near one foot six inches from the walk.

If you was to dig a hole about two feet wide and one foot deep, putting therein some good rich earth mixed with a little dung, it would be of great service to the young trees.

But let it be observed, that you do not plant trees of any kind too deep: for this is of more consequence than many people are possibly aware of.

Should you wish to plant out peach, nectarine or apricot trees, you ought to plant them at least eighteen feet distant from each other, but not too deep, as cautioned before.

Apple and pear trees being of a more vigorous and lasting growth, should be planted twenty foot or more one from the other: this distance may appear very wide at first, but they will soon extend so as to meet on the frame if your ground is good and the trees are managed in a proper manner.

RASPBERRIES

If you have not planted out as many raspberries as you would wish, this season, you may still do it; tho' the sooner this work is performed the better:—But if it is not convenient for you to execute it early in this month, you may delay it till the latter end of the next.

If you have not as yet given your old beds of raspberries their winter dressing, it should be done as

soon as possible, as the young plants will greatly improve and flourish if earthed up in proper season.

 STRAWBERRIES

If you have not put out any strawberries before now,
let the work be no longer delayed; for if the plants
are not put out early in this month, it had better be
postponed till the latter end of January, when they
will take root more freely than about Christmas.

Let the old strawberry beds be well examined if
not done in the former months, and all the dead runners and leaves be cut away, and the earth loosened
between the plants, which will strengthen them so as
to bear fine fruit the next spring.—[See November.]

ADVERTISEMENT

Robert Squibb,

 NURSERY AND SEEDSMAN;

IMPORTS annually from Europe, all the most useful kinds of Garden Grass, Flower Seeds, Roots and Tools; which he disposes of on the most reasonable terms, both at his Garden the upper-end of Tradd street, and at his Nursery near Rumney Bridge.

He also collects, and puts up (with accuracy and dispatch) all kinds of Forest Trees, Shrubs, Plants and Seeds, indigencies to the United States of America—for those who chuse to honor him with their orders.

Ladies or Gentlemen who would wish to have three or four Negro Boys (from fourteen to sixteen years of age) instructed in the modern art of Gardening, may apply as above.

SUBSCRIBERS

A

WILLIAM Ancrum, esq;
William Allston, esq;
mr. David Alexander
mr. Alexander
    Alexander
mr. James Atkins
mr. Samuel Adams
mr. James Askew
mr. Martin Alkin

B

mr. Charles Bradford
mr. Luke Breen
John Beale, esq;
General Barnwell
mr. Patrick Byrne
mr. Daniel Burger
Thomas Bourke, esq;
Peter Bonetheau, esq;

mr. Thomas Bradford
Francis Bremar, esq;
James Bentham, Esq;
Joseph Brown, Esq;
Charles Brown, esq;
mr. John Brunton
mr. William Burne
mr. J. V. Burd
mr. Charles Brown
mr. Stephen Brown
mr. James Bonsell
mr. Alexander Bethune
A. Buyer, esq;
Cornelius Blackstone,
    esq;
mr. Bass
mr. Thomas Buckle
mr. Samuel Bleakley
mr. Henry Bembridge
Thomas Bee, esq;
mrs. Eliza Blake

Peirce Butler, esq;
Joseph Bee, esq;

C

James Culliatt, esq;
David Campbell, esq;
mr. Job Colcock
mr. William Cunnington
Edward Crook, esq;
mr. John Currie
Daniel Cannon, esq;
mr. John Creighton
John E. Colhoun, esq;
mr. Thomas Coram
Macartan Campbell, esq;
mr. Thomas Cooke
Dr. George Carter
Dr. Isaac Chandler
Gabriel Capers, esq;

D

Thomas Drayton, sen.
  esq
John Dupont, esq;
John Dawson, esq;
mr. James Darby
mr. James Duncan
mr. Ralph Dawes
John L. Draper, esq;
mr. George Denner

mr. John Dorsius
mr. Joseph De Palacios
Hon. Charles Drayton
Hon. William Drayton
mr. Lewis Dutarque
John Deas, sen. esq;
John Deas, jun. esq;
mrs. Elizabeth Dewees
mr. John Dewees

D

John Edwards, jun. esq;
mr. Henry Ellison
major Edwards
mr. Richard Ellis
mr. William Eales
Thomas Elliott, esq;
mr. David Evans
Thomas O. Elliott, esq;

F

Peter Freneau, esq;
Richard Fitzgerald, esq;
Thomas Fuller, jun. esq;
Charles Ferguson, esq;
Edward Fenwick, esq;
mr. Charles Ferguson
Dr. Peter Fayssoux
Dr. James Fallon
Alexander Fraser, esq;

G

Moses Glover, esq;
William Hazell Gibbs,
 esq;
mr. John Gibbons
mr. William Graham
mr. John Walters Gibbs
mr. Robert Gibson
John Granier, esq;
James Graham, esq;
mr. John Glaze
Alexander Gillon, esq;
John Geyer, esq;
Thomas Gadsden, esq;
William Gibbs, esq;
John Lewis Gervais, esq;

H

William Hayne, esq;
Major Hambleton
Col. David Hopkins
mr. Robert Howard
mr. William Holmes
Thomas Hall, esq;
Richard J. Houston, esq;
James Harrison, esq;
Benjamin Harbinson,
 esq;
John Huger, esq;
Col. Richard Hampton

Wade Hampton, esq;
Thomas Hutchinson,
 esq;
William Huxham, esq.
Hon. Richard Hutson
Hon. Thomas Heyward
George Abbott Hall,
 esq;
Dr. Haig
Dr. Tucker Harris
General Huger

I

mr. James
mr. Charles Isaacs
Andrew Johnston, esq;
Ralph Izard, esq;
Alexander Inglis, esq;

K

Francis Kinloch, esq;

L

mr. Joseph Lasar
mr. Francis Ley
Aaron Loocock, esq;
Daniel Legare, esq;
Mrs. Jane Ladson
Benjamin Legare, esq;
mr. James Lamotte

mr. William Lee

George Lord, esq;

mr. George Lockey

Charles Lining, esq;

mr. John Leveday

James Ladion, esq;

Lambert Lance, esq;

Dr. George Logan

mr. Lewis Lestergette

PUBLISHER'S NOTE

THIS EDITION reproduces the text of the first edition, published in 1787 in Charleston, South Carolina. The eighteenth-century spelling and punctuation have been retained, imaginative and inconsistent as they may be. The only editorial changes in the text involved placing some material that had been in an appendix (February's cabbage seed and asparagus beds, and October's "garlick and shalots") in proper sequence in the calendar and restoring several characters that had dropped out of the lines of type when the 1787 edition went to press. A complete list of subscribers to the 1787 edition was not available.